Tony Brown

Jimi Hendrix
"Talking"

OMNIBUS PRESS

JIMI HENDRIX *Talking*

First published © 1994 Omnibus Press
This edition Copyright © 2003 Omnibus Press
(A Division of Music Sales Limited)

Cover & book designed by Fresh Lemon.
Picture research by Sarah Bacon.

ISBN: 1.84449.006.8
Order No: OP49588

Exclusive Distributors
Music Sales Limited, 8/9 Frith Street, London W1D 3JB, UK.

Music Sales Corporation,
257 Park Avenue South, New York, NY 10010, USA.

Macmillan Distribution Services,
53 Park West Drive, Derrimut, Vic 3030, Australia.

To the Music Trade only:
Music Sales Limited,
8/9 Frith Street, London W1D 3JB, UK.

Photo credits:
Front Cover: Gered Mankowitz; Back Cover: LFI;
Bruce Fleming/Rex Features: 100; Globe/Rex Features: 93, 108;
Harry Goodwin: 6, 17, 28, 31, 55, 88, 113; Dezo Hoffman/Rex Features: 5, 26, 68, 84, 122;
HSC/Rex Features: 117, 124; Hulton Archive: 38; K&K Ulf Kruger Ottg/Redferns: 63;
Elliott Landy/Redferns: 51; LFI: 13, 29, 32, 35, 41, 43, 44, 48, 52,
58, 60, 64, 67, 70, 74, 77, 79, 80, 83, 87, 94, 99, 104, 106, 114, 126;
David Magnus/Rex Features: 97, 121; Michael Ochs/Redferns: 18, 47, 90, 103, 118;
Barry Peake/Rex Features: 14, 128; Gunter Zint/Redferns: 111

Colour Section: Glenn A Baker Archive/Redferns: 3; Ed Caraff/Redferns: 4;
Dezo Hoffman/Rex Features: 2, 8; LFI: 6; David Redfern/Redferns: 5;
Marc Sharratt/Rex Features: 1; Gunter Zint/Redferns: 7

Every effort has been made to trace the copyright holders of the
photographs in this book but one or two were unreachable.
We would be grateful if the photographers concerned would contact us.

Printed by Caligraving Ltd, Thetford, Norfolk.

A catalogue record for this book is available from the British Library.

Visit Omnibus Press on the web at www.omnibuspress.com

CONTENTS

" My own music is in my head. If I don't get it together, nobody else will. "

Jimi Hendrix was born on November 27, 1942. His starring role as the world's most inventive rock guitarist lasted from September 1966 to September 18, 1970, the day of his tragic death in London.

On stage, Jimi Hendrix's performance was wild and extrovert, but off stage he was always unfailingly polite and shy, invariably willing to talk to anyone interested in what he had to say. Although Jimi's career was short, he gave an immense amount of interviews, particularly during his first two years of fame. On many occasions he gave two interviews or more in a day.

Introduction

Some interviewers found it a daunting task talking to Jimi Hendrix for the first time. But his on-stage reputation belied his true character, and most were pleasantly surprised by his exemplary manners, unusual shyness and good humour. This was often reflected in the headlines of the articles that followed, with lines like 'Gentleman Jimi', 'Hendrix – He's A Beautiful Person' or 'Mr Phenomenon'.

Jimi was always very articulate and unafraid to express his views. Sometimes his conversation would flow like his extraordinary guitar solos, veering off at tangents and skirting around a subject before returning to the original theme. Jimi would never use an interview as a vehicle to express his dislike for anybody, and he almost always had a complimentary word to say about everyone, especially other musicians. Sometimes Jimi would become very philosophical when confronted with someone who could grasp his complex ideas. Other interviewers, those intimidated by his honesty, were not so fortunate.

Jimi's trademark in interviews was the much over-used phrase 'You know'. Anyone remotely familiar with his interviews will recognise this phrase as an essential part of Jimi's style of personal expression, and it has been retained here. Without it, this book would not be Jimi Hendrix "Talking".

Here are Jimi's views about his life, his career, his music, his personal philosophy and his ideas for a future that unfortunately never came to pass. It's a great loss to us all that he is unable to continue to share his thoughts with us.

TONY BROWN, MARCH 1994

INTRODUCTION

Childhood

"I can remember when the nurse put on the diaper... I don't know what I was there for, but I remember when I used to wear diapers. And then she was like talking to me. She took me out of this crib, or something like that, and then she held me up to the window. This was in Seattle, and she was showing me something up against the sky, and it was fireworks and all that. It must have been the Fourth of July, you know. 'Cos then I remember her putting the diaper on me and almost sticking me, you know. I remember I didn't feel so good, you know. I must have been in the hospital sick about something. And I had a bottle and all that kinda stuff, and then she held me up to the window... she saying about a, you know... and I was looking, and the sky was just whew-whew-whew." NEW YORK, SEPTEMBER 1969

"I remember one time when I was only four and I wet my pants and I stayed out in the rain for hours, so I would get wet all over and my mum wouldn't know. She knew, though." LONDON, AUGUST 1967

"I'd be about four, I suppose. Next it was violins. I always dug string instruments and pianos. Then I started digging guitars."
TALKING ABOUT THE FIRST INSTRUMENT [A HARP] JIMI REMEMBERS
CATCHING HIS IMAGINATION. LONDON, FEBRUARY 1969

"Well, I was small enough to fit in a clothes... I remember when I was small enough to fit in a clothes basket. You know the straw clothes baskets they have in America? You put all the dirty clothes in, yeah, hampers. I remember when my cousin and I was in there playing around, about... that musta been when I was about three years old, yeah. Like sometimes when you're sitting around then you start remembering some of the things that happened beforehand. Those are the first two that come to my mind." NEW YORK, SEPTEMBER 1969

JIMI HENDRIX *Talking*

❝I used to have cats and dogs as a kid. I used to bring a stray dog home every night till my pa let me keep one. Then it was the ugliest of them all. It was really Prince Hendrix, but we just called it Dawg.❞

Dreams

❝And some dreams that I had when I was real little, you know. Like my mother was being carried away on this camel. And there was a big caravan; she's saying, 'Well I'm not gonna see ya now', and she's going under these trees, and you could see the shade, you know, the leaf patterns cross her face, when she's going under this... you know, like that. And then saying... You know how sun shines through a tree, and if you go under the shadows of a tree, the shadows go across your face; well these were in green and yellow shadows like. She's saying, 'Well, I won't be seeing you too much any more,' you know, 'so I'll see....' And then about two years after that she dies, you know. And I said, 'Yeah, but where you going?' And all like that, you know. I remember that, I always will remember that, I never did forget... there are some dreams you never forget.❞ **NEW YORK, SEPTEMBER 1969**

❝**There's this one dream you go down like that... this real big hill, but it has real long grass and then a whole lot of bananas on the floor, of the floor of this hill, but they're all spread all over, and they're growing from the ground by... each one separate. Then I remember that... and we was skating across that. I don't know how we were, but, what you do, is lay... you pour this stuff out that we made up, you know, these big bags; you pour it out across the bananas, and it fills up all the gaps, and we skate across it. 'Cos, you know, I remember those things.❞**

NEW YORK, SEPTEMBER 1969

School Days

❝I remember I used to be in school and all this, and the flies used to fly round me on a hot summer day, but it's best man to stick with it, you know❞ **FRANKFURT, MAY 1967**

❝I used to like to paint. At school the teacher used to say, 'Paint three scenes.' And I'd do abstract stuff like Martian sunsets.❞

❝School wasn't for me. According to my father I had to go working. I had done that for a few weeks with my father. He had a not-so-good running contracting firm, and in me he saw a cheap labourer. I didn't see it that way. I had to carry stones and cement all day, and he pocketed the money❞ **BELGIUM, MARCH 1967**

❝I was glad I was a high school drop-out, for the simple fact that I think kids starting from kindergarten should, every two years, have a big annual test, you know, a big test, about twenty pieces of paper, doing exactly what they want to do on that paper and saying what they want to say. And they should have people, you know, the teachers that don't want to teach for the rest of their lives, well they start... they progress too, into other things. So they'll be the instructors to this certain thing that happens every two years. And then a kid could go to school when he's eleven years old, I mean he can go to college or a special school by the time he's eleven.❞

❝Yeah, for the benefit of even the teachers, that get tired of just teaching the second grade for the rest of their lives, for instance. They could progress just like-a kids do.❞

Indians

❝I used to get so mad though, I just, you know, don't even pay too much attention... 'cos what the teachers was telling us, you know, 'Indians are bad!' I mean, you know, in other words, Indians are bad.❞ **LONDON, DECEMBER 1967**

CHILDHOOD

JIMI HENDRIX *Talking*

❝There's some of them that have a lot of money, you know, and got, you know, this and that, 'cos they get cheques and all this. But there's a lot of 'em on the reservation man, it was really terrible. Every single house is the same, you know, it's not even a house, it's like a hut. Ough! It's just a really bad scene for 'em, you know. Like half of them are down in skid row, you know, drinking and really completely out of their minds, you know, and they're not doing anything.❞ LONDON, DECEMBER 1967

❝My grandmother used to tell me beautiful Indian stories. I used to see her a lot, you know, and she used to make these clothes for me. And so then, after I stayed with her for a while, you know, I used to go back and take these clothes to school and wear them and all that and, you know, people would laugh and all this mess.**❞** LONDON, DECEMBER 1967

❝When I was small, my grandmother, she's Cherokee, gave me a little Mexican jacket with tassels. It was real good and I wore it to school every day, in spite of what people might have thought. Just because I liked it. I used to spend summer vacations on her reservation in Vancouver, and kids at school would laugh when

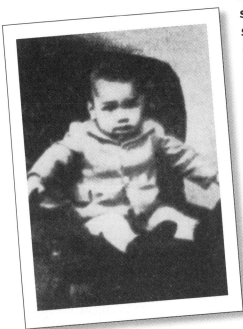

I wore shawls and poncho things she made. But on the whole my school was pretty relaxed. We had Chinese, Japanese, Puerto Ricans and Filipinos. We won all the football games! I stayed mostly at my aunt's and grandmother's. There were family troubles between my mother and father. My brother and I used to go to different homes because dad and mum used to break up all the time. Mostly my dad took care of me. He was a labourer, a gardener, and he'd once been an electrician, but we weren't too rich!❞ LONDON, OCTOBER 1967

WITH HIS FATHER, AL

First Guitar

❝I learned to play on a guitar which belonged to one of my father's friends who came to play cards. While the two men played, I would creep out onto the porch with the friend's guitar and see what I could get out of it. I didn't know that I would have to put the strings round the other way, because I was left-handed, but it just didn't feel right. I can remember thinking to myself, 'There's something wrong here.'❞

❝One night my dad's friend was stoned and he sold me the guitar for five dollars. I changed the strings round but it was way out of tune when I'd finished. I didn't know a thing about tuning so I went down to the store and run my fingers across the strings on a guitar they had there. After that I got tired of the guitar and put it aside. But when I heard Chuck Berry, it revived my interest. I learned all the riffs I could.❞

First Band

❝I formed this group with some other guys, but they drowned me out. I didn't know why at first, but after about three months I realised I'd have to get an electric guitar. Well it's so very hard to me, 'cos at first man I was so scared, I wouldn't dare go on stage, no, you know, like I joined this band, I knew about three songs and when it's time for us to play on stage man, I was like this [shaking gesture], you know, and then I had to

JIMI WITH THE KING CASUALS, IN 1963. FEATURING BILLY COX (BASS - CENTRE) AND LEONARD MOSES (GUITAR - RIGHT)

play behind the curtains, you know, I couldn't get up in front... then plus you get very discouraged; you hear different bands playing around you and the guitar player seems like he's always much better then you are, you know. Then most people give up at this point because, you know, they get very discouraged, but it's best not to, you know, just keep on, just keep on, if you're very stubborn you can, you know, make it; that's the only way I, you know... try to make it is being very persistent. **"**

FRANKFURT, MARCH 1967

First Electric Guitar

"My first was a Danelectro [this was Jimi's second guitar] which my dad bought for me; must have busted him for a long time. I first had to prove that I could play a couple of songs on a guitar of a friend, but I did still get it. **"** BELGIUM, MARCH 1967

First Gig

"I remember my first gig was at an armoury, a National Guard place, and we earned 35 cents apiece. In those days I just liked rock-and-roll, I guess. We used to play stuff by people like The Coasters. **"**

LONDON, FEBRUARY 1969

"We played on the West Coast and in Washington and down South. We had guys ten years ago in the States playing what groups are playing here now. Now they call it psychedelic. "

CHILDHOOD **"**

Army Days

"Because I didn't have a cent in my pocket, I walked into the first recruitment office I saw and went into the Army."

"**The Army really taught me what boredom is. There's nothing more monotonous than spending a whole day peeling potatoes.**"

LONDON, JUNE 1967

"I did have one bad time in the South. When I was in the Army and got stationed in Kentucky about nine months. Well, Kentucky's right on the border of North and South and in that camp were some of the orneriest, most boot-licking guys. Some of the officers... Man it was terrible."

Parachuting

"Oh the first jump is really outtasight, like you're in this plane, you know, some cats has never been in a plane before, somebody would be throwing up in a... you've got a big bucket, you know, big garbage can sitting in the middle, it was great. At the beginning the plane is going roarrrrrr, this roaring and shaking and you can see the rivets is jumping around... talking about what am I doing here. We'd have to start from the third person down though, you know, I used to watch 'em and said, 'Wow', a split second thought went through me like, 'you're crazy,' and all of a sudden it just disappeared. And it's almost like blank and it's almost like a crying and you wanna laugh, and you pat the sergeant on the back, say, 'Ha ha, who's this joker who wants to be Sarge?' But you knowing all the time, you know, you say, 'What the hell am I doing here.' And by that time, you're just there at the door, and all of a sudden,

JIMI HENDRIX *Talking*

PRIVATE J. M. HENDRIX (AGE 18), FORT ORD, CALIFORNIA

you know, this flat rush, and all of a sudden then you're up like that, and then you're just ohhhhhhh... Physically it was a very, very, you know, falling over backwards feeling in your dreams. It's so personal 'cos once you're out there, everything is so quiet, all you can hear is the breeze going shhhhhsh, you know, like that. You're there all by yourself, and you can talk very low, you can scream or anything, and I think how crazy I was for doing this thing, but I loved it anyway. And then you're supposed to look up, you know, and you see if your chute is open, and if it's open, and then you can say, 'Thank the Lord.'" **LONDON, DECEMBER 1967**

"I was in the Army for about 13 months, you know, 'cos I got tired of that and it was very boring, and so I pretended that I hurt my back, you know, and I really did break my ankle. So I got out like that, you know." STOCKHOLM, MAY 1967

"I joined the Army Airborne and got to Spec 4 – that's what you would call a corporal – but I got injured on a jump and hung up on the discipline. One day I got my ankle caught in the sky-hook just as I was going to jump, and I broke it. I told them I'd hurt my back too. Every time they examined me I groaned, so they finally believed me and I got out." **LONDON, AUGUST 1967**

"Anyway, my discharge came through, and one morning, I found myself standing outside the gates at Fort Campbell, on the Tennessee–Kentucky border with my

duffle bag and three or four hundred dollars in my pocket. I was going to go back to Seattle, which was a long way away, but there was this girl there I was kinda hung up on. Then I thought I'd just look in at Clarksville, which was near; stay there the night and go home next morning. That's what I did, looked in at Clarksville. I went in this jazz joint and had a drink, liked it and stayed. I came out of that place with sixteen dollars left, and it takes a lot more than that to get from Tennessee to Seattle. All I can do I thought is get a guitar and try to find work here. **"**

"I remembered that just before I left the Army, I'd sold a guitar to a cat in my unit. So I went back to Fort Campbell and slept there on the sly that night. I found the guy and told him I just had to borrow the guitar back. **"**

"All I can really remember is like, getting out of the Army and then trying to get something together, and then I was playing in different groups all over the States, you know, and Canada; playing behind people most of the times. **"** LONDON, JANUARY 1969

ARMY DAYS

The Early Bands

Clarksville

❝I moved to Clarksville where the group I was with worked for a set-up called W&W. Man, they paid us so little that we decided that the two Ws stood for wicked and wrong.❞

Nashville

❝Then we got in with a club owner, who seemed to like us a lot. He bought us some new gear. I had a Silvertone amp and the other got Fender Band Masters. But this guy took our money and he was sort of holding us back. The promoters were the strangest and the most crooked there [Nashville]. They used to come right up on to this makeshift stage while we were in the middle of a number, slip our money into our pockets and disappear. Then we'd find out afterwards that they'd only slipped us a couple of dollars instead of ten or fifteen. We used to have to sleep in a big housing estate they were building around there. No roofs and sometimes they hadn't put floors in yet. That was wild! Nashville used to be a pretty funny scene, with all those slick managers trying to sign up hillbilly singers who'd never been in a big town before.❞

LONDON, SEPTEMBER 1967

JIMI WITH CURTIS KNIGHT (FRONT CENTRE)
AND THE SQUIRES, 1965

JIMI HENDRIX *Talking*

JIMI HENDRIX *Talking*

> **I started playing around all over the South, you know. We had a band in Nashville, Tennessee, and I got tired of playing that 'cos, you know, they don't want to move anywhere. They just want to stay there.** STOCKHOLM, MAY 1967

> In the bars I used to play in, we'd get up on the platform where the fan was, in one of them nice, hot, greasy, funky clubs. We'd play up there, and it was really hot, and the fan is making love to you. And you really had to play, 'cos those people were really hard to please. It was one of the hardest audiences in the South; they hear it all the time. Everybody knows how to play guitar. You walk down the street and people are sitting on their porch playing more guitar. That's where I learned to play, really, in Nashville.
>
> **HOLLYWOOD, AUGUST 1967**

> **I was in Nashville, Tennessee for quite a while and every afternoon we didn't have anything to do, we'd go downtown and watch the fights. Yeah, it can get pretty bad down there.**

The Isley Brothers

> So I started travelling around and I went to New York and won first place in the Apollo Amateur Contest, you know... twenty-five dollars and so I stayed up there or starved up there for about two or three weeks. Then I got... Isley Brothers asked... you know, The Isley Brothers? The ones with 'Twist & Shout', asked if I'd like to, you know, play with them. So I play with them for a while, and it got very boring, you know, 'cos you get very tired playing behind other people all the time, you know. So then I quit, you know, I quit them in Nashville somewhere. **STOCKHOLM, MAY 1967**

> **When I was with The Isley Brothers, they used to make me do my thing then, because it made them more bucks or something, I don't know, anyway with them. But I used to like to do it then; but most of the groups I was with then, didn't let me do my own thing, you know, like feedback and 'Midnight Hour' and something like that.** LONDON, JANUARY 1969

❝I had to conform when I was playing in groups too. The so-called grooming bit. You know, mohair suits, how I hate mohair suits! I was playing with The Isley Brothers and we had white mohair suits, patent leather shoes and patent leather hair-do's. We weren't allowed to go on stage looking casual. If our shoe laces were two different types we'd get fined five dollars. Oh man, did I get tired of that!❞ **LONDON, FEBRUARY 1967**

JIMI WITH THE ROCKING KINGS, 1960 (L-R LESTER EXKANO (DRUMS), JIMI (GUITAR), WEB LAFTON AND WALTER HARRIS (HORNS) AND ROBERT GREEN (PIANO)

The Chitlin Circuit

❝I worked with this guy, we was on tour with B.B. King, Jackie Wilson and Sam Cooke, you know, and all these people... Chuck Jackson. So I played... was playing guitar behind a lot of the acts on the tour and then I got stranded in Kansas City, 'cos I missed the bus, you know.❞ **STOCKHOLM, MAY 1967**

THE EARLY BANDS

" Steve Cropper turned me on millions of years ago and I turned him on millions of years ago too, but because of different songs. Like we went into the studio and we started teaching each other. I found him at the soul restaurant eating all this stuff right across from the studio in Memphis. I was playing on this top 40 R&B Soul Hit Parade package with the patent leather shoe and hair-do's combined.

WITH CURTIS KNIGHT AND BAND AT
THE CHEETAH CLUB, NEW YORK, MAY 1966

So anyway I got into the studio and said, 'Hey man, dig, I heard you're all right; that anyone can come down here if they've got a song.' So we went into the studio and did a song and after that it was just guitar and he was messing around with the engineering and it's just a demo acetate. I don't know where it is now. After we did that, we messed around the studio for four or five hours doing different things, it was very strange. He turned me on to a lot of things. He showed me how to play certain songs and I showed him how I played 'Mercy, Mercy' or something like that. " NEW YORK, FEBRUARY 1968

Little Richard

❝So I was in Kansas City, Missouri, and didn't have any money, then some group, you know, this group came up and brought me back to Atlanta, Georgia, where I met Little Richard and I started playing with him for a while.❞ **STOCKHOLM, MAY 1967**

❝**I guess I played with him for about six months I guess, about five or six months, and I got tired with that, you know, and played some shows with Ike & Tina Turner. And then I went back to New York and played with King Curtis and Joey Dee, you know. I was playing with... but all the time I was playing behind these different groups.**❞ STOCKHOLM, MAY 1967

❝I had these dreams that something was gonna happen, seeing the number 1966 in my sleep. So I was just passing time till then. I wanted my own scene, making my music, not playing the same riffs. Like once with Little Richard, me and another guy got fancy shirts 'cos we were tired of wearing the uniform. Richard called a meeting. 'I am Little Richard, I am Little Richard,' he said, 'the King of Rock and Rhythm, I am the only one allowed to be pretty. Take off those shirts.' Man, it was all like that. Bad pay, lousy living, and getting burned.❞

❝**I went through all of America with him [Little Richard]. In Los Angeles I had enough of Richard, and played in the band of Ike and Tina Turner.**❞ BELGIUM, MARCH 1967

Joey Dee & The Starlighters

❝I played Cleveland before man, with Joey Dee at the Arena in some rhythm and blues show that had Chubby Checker in it. Nobody talked to me. I was just another Negro artist, I was here three years ago with Chuck Jackson and all. No one noticed, then.❞ **STOCKHOLM, MAY 1967**

THE EARLY BANDS

Curtis Knight & The Squires

"Then I played with this little rhythm and blues group named Curtis Knight & The Squires. And I made a few records and arranged a few songs for him. And I just got tired where I just couldn't stand any more. So I just went down to the Village and got my own little group together named The Rainflowers, you know. We had two names, The Rainflowers, and The Blue Flames, you know, any one of those names was all right." STOCKHOLM, MAY 1967

Greenwich Village

"I was playing behind different acts like... you know, like... what is it, Little Richard, Isley Brothers, you know, and some shows with Tina Turner and Hank Ballard, you know, Chuck Jackson; the regular top forty R&B and... you know, you get kinda tired of playing the same songs all the time and so I was just... you know, I went down to the Village in New York, Greenwich Village and had a little group together down there named The Rainflowers and then we changed about a thousand times." FRANKFURT, MAY 1967

"I was down in the Village, it was right before I quit this R&B group, you know, 'cos I said, 'well come on down to the Village so we can get something together,' you know, on our own standards, not playing behind another person that we was playing behind. And they were lazy, they were scared and plus, they didn't think they was gonna get paid. I said, 'well quite naturally you won't get paid on audition,' you know, because like it's us, and, you know, going down there and being aggressive, you know, it's us going up filtering down to them, you know. So here's a few things you have to give up at the beginning. They don't wanna do that, so I just went down there and played. Got Randy California together and formed this group called The Blue Flames."

"You know, you get tired of playing other people's music all the time. So then I just, you know, I went down to the Village, you know, just laying dead for a while playing... So he [Chas Chandler] asked would I like to go to England, you know. I wasn't doing anything so I said yeah.**"**

"I'd never been to England before, so I decided to go over there. Before we went over there, we was having offers, this other group that I had, you know, with Randy California, the guitar player of the Spirit now. So the group we had in the Village, like we got offers from Columbia, Epic, you know, the regular scene, you know. But I didn't feel, well we was completely ready then, not as a group, not that type of group. I just happened to go, you know, to England 'cos these cats asked me to come over there."

MINNEAPOLIS, NOVEMBER 1968

JIMI WITH CURTIS KNIGHT AND BAND, 1965 **THE EARLY BANDS**

From The Experience & Beyond

The Formation Of The Experience

"One of the managers of The Animals... you know, The Animals were in town one time doing their last gig at Central Park, doing their last gig as a group. And the bass player of The Animals, Chas Chandler, and Mike Jeffery, asked if I'd like to come to England. And I'd never been to England before, that's the only reason, 'cos I'd never been. So I went over there, 'cos that's why I just live my life. I'd never been to Indianapolis, so I starve my way over there. I'd never been to, you know, Memphis, so I'll starve my way down there. It just happened to happen over there, that's all. And plus I could play louder over there, I could really get myself together over there. There wasn't so many hang-ups as there was in America, you know, mental hang-ups and, things like that. Chas [Chandler] came down one time, 'cos he's... they were playing in Central Park Festival and he came down and heard us and asked if I'd like to come to England, you know, so I said 'yeah, you know, yeah I'd like to come,' so we came over here." FRANKFURT, MAY 1967

"I was going with this girl, you know... had this girlfriend from England that I met from one of the clubs in New York. And she told Chas about me, 'cos Chas... you know, The Animals were

THE JIMI HENDRIX EXPERIENCE WITH
NOEL REDDING (SEATED) AND MITCH MITCHELL

JIMI HENDRIX *Talking*

playing in Central Park.
So he came down and heard
me, you know, and asked if
I would like to come over to
England and start a group
over here, over to England.
And I said yeah, you know.
So I came over to England
and met Mitch and Noel,
you know, Noel Redding
the bass player and Mitch
Mitchell the drummer. "
STOCKHOLM, MAY 1967

MITCH MITCHELL

"And then we had a jam
session, at some club in
England, and that's how Mitch, Noel and I got together.
Noel comes down expecting to play guitar, you know, he was trying
for The Animals, so I dug his hair style, so asked him to play
bass. " LONDON, JANUARY 1969

**"Mitch Mitchell the drummer, you know, and Noel Redding the
bass player and I, we got together and formed our group, and
you know, it's been happening ever since. "** HOLLYWOOD, JULY 1967

"Mitch Mitchell, yeah, he used to play with Georgie Fame of
The Blue Flames, and Noel Redding used to be in a group named
The Loving Kind, and The Burnettes, you know, and he used to play
guitar until he came down... he came down for the audition for
The New Animals with his guitar, you know, and Chas asked him to
play the bass... try at playing the bass, and he's been playing the
bass ever since, and it's worked out, you know, perfect. And Mitch,
he's about the best out of about twenty drummers we heard. "
STOCKHOLM, MAY 1967

**"It's all happened thanks to Chas and Mike [Jeffery] really.
They were the ones who really had the faith that I could make it
over here. I was hopeful, but not that confident. I was just**

playing with my own group in Greenwich Village when Chas saw me. He said it would all happen, just like he said. I still find it difficult to believe it's all happened so fast. I'm working so hard, I guess I don't have time to think about it. Once you make a name for yourself, you are all the more determined to keep it up. In any case, I don't believe you've really made it until you breathe your last breath! So what we are trying to do is to be more and more progressive, to make our music and our act more varied and exciting and interesting, so that all age groups can enjoy it. We didn't do too much, you know. I couldn't work too much 'cos I didn't have a work permit, so what they did was line up a lot of gigs, so when we did the first... one of the first jobs we ever did was... we had about four hours practice, and Johnny Halliday asked whether we would like to come to... you know, play at the Paris Olympia with him, and we did after being together only about four days and after having about four hours of practice. **"**

STOCKHOLM, MAY 1967

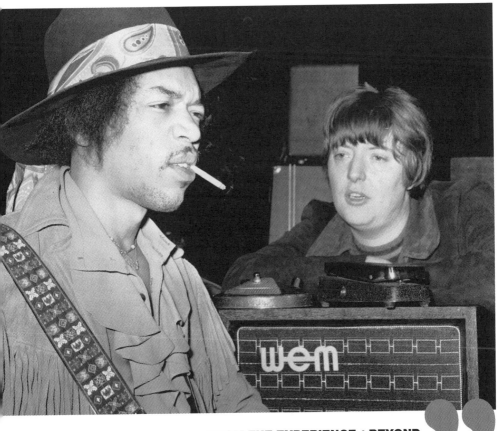

JIMI WITH CHAS CHANDLER, 1969   **FROM THE EXPERIENCE & BEYOND**

JIMI HENDRIX *Talking*

"Like we tried an organ, maybe, what was it? About fifteen minutes and it just didn't work out there. It made us sound like just anybody, anybody in the street, you know, I mean, to us it made us sound like that. But it isn't ideal this in a trio, 'cos of certain... some different numbers, and all; they just happened like that. But like, we'd like to put on a completely different presentation and all that. You know, I can't say any more about that though, you know, from, like pop itself say for instance around maybe the summer, the late summer or fall or something like that. We want a completely different presentation to it." **NEW YORK, JANUARY 1968**

"**All three of us, we like... we all have our own little scenes as far as music. Noel likes, you know, nice gutsy rock, you know, and he plays guitar, you know, he's been playing bass only since he's been with us. And then like Mitch plays a whole lot of drums.**"
NEW YORK, JANUARY 1968

The Break Up Of The Experience

"What we're doing, we're gonna get ready to do our own individual things. Like, for instance, Noel Redding, he's writing some songs with another person, and like, you'll probably see him on stage with his group. And then you'll probably see Mitch with his thing, you know, and then you might even see me with my thing, you know. It's three individual things we'd like to do, but plus, well, keep the group together, because we haven't fully discovered all the sounds and all the things we want to do with a three-piece group, you know. So I don't know how that got around, but like, I don't plan for us to split up, not really. Not until we really bore ourselves." **SWEDEN, JANUARY 1969**

"**Well, we're gonna have to make fewer personal appearances, because like, we haven't had a rest since we've been together, you know. And like, we're gonna have to take a rest sometime or another, or else our**

NOEL REDDING

music's gonna come out really, really, you know, bad, or it's not gonna come out proper, the way we want it to. So you have to have proper rest; mental rest too, before you can really create nice sounds and music." SWEDEN, JANUARY 1969

"But there's no definite break-up thing like that. We might work a little less, but our records will be better, you know, because we'll have better peace of mind, you know. See, 'cos I get very bored regardless of how good anybody else is, and I'm sure every other people might get bored too. It's like I get bored myself. I'm, you know... it's... I can't play guitar any more the way I want to. You know, I get very frustrated sometimes on stage, when we play. And I think it's because it's only three pieces, you know. I like to work with other things too, and I'm sure they would too, you know. But that doesn't necessarily mean we have to break the group up." **SWEDEN, JANUARY 1969**

"My Jimi Hendrix Experience will not be disbanded. What rubbish. We used to pluck strings through our gigs for starvation wages. We cannot have it better than today. As a musical trinity we are unbeatable." BERLIN, JANUARY 1969

"There's a certain period of music that's happening this very instant and it's gonna go on happening for about, maybe about another month or two, you know, and like it's a frustration period, it's a change over from the, what do you call it? The primitive rock scene, you know, to a progressive rock. Like our drummer Mitch, he's going through that scene too, you know, he's going through a scene as it were, he's such an excellent drummer that he doesn't know which way to go; well he knows probably, but like, for a

FROM THE EXPERIENCE & BEYOND

three-piece group, well it's very hard to try to... you know, like make the jazz really come out good and then make the blues really come out good and make the rock really come out good. So like we're gonna get our own groups together you know and plus keep our group together. So I think that concept is great, once we practise, you know, I mean well not practise, but once we start playing a lot. **"** LONDON, FEBRUARY 1969

The Sky Church Band

" We're just getting ourselves together. We're going to play mostly outside places that hold a lot of people, you know. It'll be like a Sky Church sort of thing. You can get all your answers through music anyway, and the best way is through open air. We're going to play a lot of places, like in the ghettos in Harlem and so forth. Free when we can. Most of them would be on donation though. It'll be up to the people. **"**

BEVERLY HILLS, JUNE 1969

" The new thing will consist of writers too. We're going to have Albert Allen writing songs, from the twins. He has a brother who's getting himself together now, getting his own self together, which everybody should go through anyway. That's part of what we're going to be preaching. There's a lot of things we might be saying that people might want to escape the truth of, and base it on good and bad. But it's not actually the idea between good and bad; it's just true and false. We'll be on a truth kick. **"** BEVERLY HILLS, JUNE 1969

"I don't like the name Church, because it sounds too funky, too sweaty. You think of a person praying between his legs on the ground. So until we find something better, we'll have to use that, you know, so we can keep identification some kind of way, while we create a new one. You see, it's best not to harp upon us, the personalities and all that. It's the whole thing; what the whole thing is trying to get across. I'd like to get a hold of the Buddy Miles group, and call them the 'Freedom Express' featuring Buddy Miles. Billy would be our bass player. I'd like to get three 'Soul Sisters', regardless of whether they're Italian or Irish or whatever, so long as they got feeling, it's feeling first. We have this family type thing we are trying to get together, and then the money thing will come. Nowadays too many musicians think of the money and the image first, before they figure out what they're trying to get across. But we already know the hang-ups." **BEVERLY HILLS, JUNE 1969**

"This new thing, we'll try a little bit of it in Harlem, at the Apollo Theater. That'll be around July 11. That'll be a chance. It isn't completely together yet, but it's good like this. I'd rather experiment up there than down in the Village, because you get, what do you call it? Stagnant; you get very bad scenes down there; everybody cops off each other, so you don't get nothing real. You go uptown to hear real music in the first place. Now the job is to get those people uptown together. Once we get everybody together, there's so many things happening."

BEVERLY HILLS, JUNE 1969

A Band Of Gypsys

"They can get it together if they want to. The whole world is their front porch. Musically we try to keep it together. That's why we have to change. That's why personnels in groups always change all the time. 'Cos they're always constantly searching for that certain little thing. The fact of calling it Gypsys means it could even expand on personnel or so forth and so on. And it's just going to be laying down what we see today. How we see things today.

FROM THE EXPERIENCE & BEYOND "

It's no big problem. We have one song in there called 'Sky Blues Today'. It's nothing but electronic blues, electric blues and rock. It's all bottom. It's all rhythm. We're working on our voices. Buddy is getting all the voices together where that will be another instrument. ❞

NEW YORK, DECEMBER 1969

❝We would like to plan a tour. We'd like to be on the major festivals. We'll play anywhere, where we know it's gonna make some kind of penetration or some kind of impact. Anywhere! We can play at the Whiskey, and then we'll play at the Hollywood Bowl. We'll play at all the funky clubs. I mean, we could. We're gearing ourselves so we could play anywhere. I might not even be there all the time. Buddy might not even be there all the time, but the core, the whole, the child will be there!❞

NEW YORK, DECEMBER 1969

The End Of The Gypsys – The End Of a Big Long Fairy Tale

❝I don't know, it's like, it's the end of a beginning maybe, or something. I figure that Madison Square Garden was like the end of a big long fairy tale, you know? Which is great, you know. I think it was the best ending I can possibly come up with. The band was out of sight as far as I'm concerned. It was another... it was just something with head changes; going through changes. It just happened to catch me at that particular time. I was very tired. You know, sometimes there's a lot of things that add up into your head about this and that. And they might hit you at a very peculiar time, which happened to be at that peace rally, you know, and here I am fighting the biggest war I ever fought in my life, inside, you know. And like that wasn't the place to do it. ❞

NEW YORK, FEBRUARY 1970

The Re-formation Of The Experience That Was Not To Be

"Right now I'm just concentrating on, you know, for us to get back together again.**"** **NEW YORK, FEBRUARY 1970**

"Well we're gonna take some time off and go out somewhere in the hills or in the woodshed or whatever you call it, you know; to get some new songs and new arrangements and so forth together, so we'd have something to offer, you know, something new, regardless if it's different or not; but get something together." NEW YORK, FEBRUARY 1970

FROM THE EXPERIENCE & **BEYOND**

JIMI HENDRIX *Talking*

" I'm the only one that needs to be experience anyway, you know, but, you know, instead of the smishmosh or missmosh. Between Madame Flipflop and her all-night social workers. **"**

NEW YORK, FEBRUARY 1970

"Like about putting other groups on the tour, you know, like our friends or whatever. I don't know about that right now, not at a stage like this; 'cos we're in the process of, you know, getting our own thing together now, as far as a group; far as a three-piece group. But like eventually I guess... you know, like if we have time on the side, that's like, as Noel was talking about, we have a scheduled time. We have time on the side to play with your friends and all. That's why I'll always be... you know, I'll probably be jamming with Buddy and Billy, probably be recording too on the side, and they'll be doing the same." NEW YORK, FEBRUARY 1970

" I'd like for it to be permanent. Well, things don't have to be official all the time, you know. Things don't have to be formal or official, you know, you can have jams and stuff. It's just like jamming. It's just like... you know, we have a schedule. This band will be like my main concern because this is, you know, as far as I'm concerned it's what's happening. **"** **NEW YORK, FEBRUARY 1970**

"The longest we ever played together, is when we're on stage. We played about two and a half hours; three hours once. Almost three hours one time. On a gig." NEW YORK, FEBRUARY 1970

After The Split With Billy Cox – A Man Without A Band

" I really don't know what kind of band to continue with. I think I'll get another small one together I guess. It's really hard to decide, you know, I'd like to have both if I could. Like use one for touring and then sometimes I could do another tour with the big one, you know, whatever. But it all depends, you know. It's really hard to

37

know what people want around here sometimes. All I'm gonna do is just go on and do what I feel, but, like right now I don't... I can't feel anything right now because like there's a few things that's just happened, you know, and so like, I just have to like, lay back and think about it all. **LONDON, SEPTEMBER 1970**

Well, there was a period when I stopped talking so much, because like, you know; just going through certain things here and there, and like... Oh, I don't know, really. It was just... I guess it was something else to talk about or something, whatever. 'Cos like I just got very quiet for a while. I just like, you know, just did the gigs and just like stayed in, and tried to stay away and all that, you know. It was probably one of those things. 'Cos like I was changing. I felt like I was changing and getting into like heavier music and it was getting unbearable with the three pieces, you know. And like I always wanted to expand and all this, but I think I'll go back to three pieces again now. And get another bass player, and I'll probably be loud again.

LONDON, SEPTEMBER 1970

I think it would count more, if we did less, you know, personal appearances. We're trying to get a tour of England together now, but like, that's definitely gonna call for another bass player. **LONDON, SEPTEMBER 1970**

I'd probably get very wild though and wrapped up into that other scene again, you know, like with the hair and so forth, or the visuals, probably. LONDON, SEPTEMBER 1970

Well that's exactly what I wanna do, actually. That's what I have to do. All I do is get like... probably get a two guitars, counting myself, and an organist and a singer, you know, and drums, quite naturally, and bass. If I can get something like that, that would be out of sight. **LONDON, SEPTEMBER 1970**

FROM THE EXPERIENCE & BEYOND

Life on the Road

Miming

❝The one thing I really hate is miming, it's so phoney. So far, the only thing I was asked to mime was a Radio London appearance and I felt guilty just standing there holding a guitar.❞

The Walker Brothers Tour

❝Most will come to see the Walkers. Those who come to see Engelbert sing 'Release Me', may not dig me, but that's not tragic. We'll play for ourselves, we've done it before, where the audience stands about with their mouths open and you wait ten minutes before they clap.❞

❝The tour manager (Don Finlayson) told me to stop using all this in my act, because he said it was obscene and vulgar. I have been threatened every night of the tour so far and I'm not going to stop for him. There's nothing vulgar about it at all. I've been using this act all the way since I've been in Britain. I just don't know where these people get the idea from that it's an obscene act.❞

JIMI HENDRIX *Talking*

The Monkees Tour

"Firstly they gave us the 'death' spot on the show, right before The Monkees were due on. The audience just screamed and yelled for The Monkees! Finally they agreed to let us go on first and things were much better. We got screams and good reactions, and some kids even rushed the stage. But we were not getting any billing. All the posters on the show just screamed out MONKEES. Then some parents who brought their young kids complained that our act was vulgar. We decided it was just the wrong audience. I think they're replacing me with Mickey Mouse."

England Versus America

"Well actually, we've only worked over there [America] once. Like when we were there, it's about the same as over here. Like, as far as receptions, they really gave us nice receptions. Every place we played was a complete success; and there's really no difference at all except that they know more about us over here than they do over there. Now they're starting to catch on to us over there. So, it's the time." **LONDON, DECEMBER 1967**

"[England] It's a little more together as far as musicians and all that, you know, 'cos they work a little more, you know, they know all each other, 'cos it's a small place, you know, and everybody congregates around London, the main thing. There isn't all that much difference though really, 'cos they have their own scene and, you know, they got their own scene over here."

NEW YORK, JANUARY 1968

"I like to jam a lot, you know, and they don't do that too much over there, [England] not too much. I like to play with other cats, you know, and like I say play with other people, you know. A lot of ideas that I have, well you just can't do them over there sometimes." **NEW YORK, JANUARY 1968**

"I couldn't even compare it, we don't think like that. Like, they're quieter over there. [England] They listen very, very close; that's one thing I have to say, you know. They listen very close and then they show their appreciation after you finish a number."

NEW YORK, JANUARY 1968

Playing In America

"I love to play in Texas. Texas and Florida. I don't know why. Maybe it's the weather, and the feeling of it, you know. The South is... you know, I dig the South a little more than playing in the North. It's more of a pressure playing in the Mid-West, you know, like Cleveland or Chicago. It's very... you know, it's like being in a pressure cooker, waiting for the top to blow off. The people there are groovy, but it's just the atmosphere or something, you know. Down South is great. New Orleans? That's great. Like Arizona, that's great. Arizona is fantastic. It's great playing in Utah, you know, the colleges and all those places. Well, the people, you know, once we're off stage it's another world, but like the people  **are great though, you know. But like when we play at the gigs, they was really listening, they was really tuned in some kind of way or another. I think it was the air. People make sounds when they clap, some of them make sounds back. I like electric sounds, feedback and so forth, static."**

 **JIMI HENDRIX** *Talking*

Touring

“It's outasight, it's really good, you know, we're getting through to a lot of people that we normally wouldn't have if we wasn't on tour.**”** **MINNEAPOLIS, NOVEMBER 1968**

“As long as we get through to 'em, you know. The first initial thing is like... It's always like... they sound surprised a lot of the times at first. And then we come through again, you know. Most people just hit it off just like that because they've heard about us before. But it's groovy to play to people who listen.”

MINNEAPOLIS, NOVEMBER 1968

“And the response is always afterwards, and they show their appreciation in all groovy ways, you know, you can feel it when you're on stage, even though you can't see 'em all the time.**”**

MINNEAPOLIS, NOVEMBER 1968

“We don't judge by the people, you know. We go by how well we get across maybe... like for instance music-wise, you know. If we're not laying down anything and they're screaming and hollering and thinking that's good, well then that makes you feel bad.”

“They're just freaking out when we play, but they listen though which is a groovy thing, you know, when the audience is quiet while you're playing, that's really great, that means they're listening. That's like around Canada is listening, you know, there's a few little piggies in the back row, you know, squealing here and there once in a while, but I don't know, I don't think about those things, I think about, you know, their feeling that is there, it's like all the spirits like collect for an hour and a half or so, that's the way it's supposed to be, it doesn't call for talking and yelling then, does it?**”** **LONDON, JANUARY 1969**

“It's very hard sometimes. If you look out there and see. If there's about two hundred people in front of you, you know good and well that those people way out there are not going to hear

anything. Unless we're down at the Bowl. I had a lot of fun at the Denver, Colorado, place. We played out there at Red Rocks, that was groovy, that was nice 'cos people are on top of you there, or at least they can hear something. That's where it should be, natural theatre-type things.** NEW YORK, DECEMBER 1969

IN ZURICH, FOR THE BEAT MONSTERS CONCERT, MAY 1968, WITH MEMBERS OF
ERIC BURDON AND THE ANIMALS, EIRE APPARENT, JOHN MAYALL, THE MOVE AND TRAFFIC

Well, I really feel like... I don't know, I really feel like turning people on, you know, quite naturally, on some kind... at least entertainment, without being false about it, you know, without being, a superficial clown or whatever you want to call it, I don't know. And like if they don't respond, well, then I'll just play for myself, you know, and for the ones that will listen. If they do respond, well, then this gives me more energy to work out, you know. It's another way of communication and trying to make harmony amongst the people enjoying what we're trying to get across, you know. Harmony's part of the first one too anyway.

BEVERLY HILLS, JUNE 1969

LIFE ON THE ROAD

**❝I'm so glad that people
are looking at our music
a little more than just the
average... you know, a
little more than just a fad.
And I feel really respected
to do something like
this.❞** BEVERLY HILLS, JUNE 1969

❝I have an imagination,
you know, and I feel that
maybe they're not... they
might not be ready for
that particular thing then;
they might be coming to
the concert as critics, you
know, instead of as people, you know, wanting to
get into some entertainment and then from then on we can build it
more. But like if there's no response at all, it doesn't bother me too
much at all, it just makes me play a little more music, you know.
See that's just the way I think; I think in no negative terms at all,
'cos it takes up a whole lot of space in your mind, you know. And
some people only use one tenth of their brain capacity anyway.
And so, you know, there's so much more room to think other good
ways, you know, and try to turn them on regardless 'cos it's like a
hospital, when a patient might be kicking, you know, he doesn't
want an operation and he knows good and well, you know, it might
be good for him in the long run, but he's scared and he's kicking
around in the bed and the nurses are trying to strap him down.
Well, I'm the nurses, you know, trying to get him together and
trying to prove to him that this is right.**❞ BEVERLY HILLS, JUNE 1969**

Festivals

❝This summer's going to do that about twice as big. Three times...
I bet they're going to have more than a million at least, at one or
two of those festivals this summer. Like I say, as long as it's done

up for the idea of enjoying and picking up on good vibes. Monterey was great. It was a predominantly music festival done up the way it's supposed to be done up. That's our start in America. I didn't know too much about festivals and all that, except I used to go down there at jazz festivals. Beyond that, it was great. I was scared to go up there and play in front of all those people outside. Everything was perfect. In other words, I was scared at that almost. I said, 'Wow! Everything's together! What am I gonna do.'"

NEW YORK, DECEMBER 1969

"You really want to turn those people on. It's just like a feeling of really deep concern. You get very intense. That's the way I look at it. That's natural for me. Once you hit the first note, or once the first thing goes down, then it's all right." NEW YORK, DECEMBER 1969

"Let's get to those people's butts! That's what I want. We used to say things like, 'If you don't have no blues with you, we'll make some to take home.' That's going to be our theme. Not sad blues, you know... blues today." NEW YORK, DECEMBER 1969

Woodstock

"The non-violence. The very, very, very good brand of music, I don't mean good, I mean the very true brand of music, where acceptance of the long awaited crowd, how they've had to sleep in the mud and rain and get hassled by this, hassled by that and still come through saying that it was a successful festival. That's what it is, you know, that's one of the good things. There's so many scores you can add up on this thing; if you added them all up, you know, you feel like a king. They're tired of joining the street gangs, they're tired of joining militant groups, they're tired of hearing the President gab his gums away. They're tired of this, tired of that, they want to find different direction. They know they're on the right track, but where in the hell is it coming from?"

WOODSTOCK, AUGUST 1969

LIFE ON THE ROAD

JIMI HENDRIX *Talking*

"That's what it's all about, you know, is draw... try to keep violence down, you know, keep 'em off the streets, and like a festival of five-hundred-thousand people was a very beautiful turn out, you know. I hope we have more of 'em, you know, it'd be nice." NEW YORK, SEPTEMBER 1969

"It was a success for the simple fact that there was one of the largest gatherings of people, you know, in a musical sense of it, you know? And it could have been arranged a little more, you know, a little more tighter, but it was a complete success though, compared to all the other festivals that everybody tried to knock here and there, you know. I'd like to see the same thing happen in the... see some kind of chartered bus thing come from different areas of town, you know 'cos I'd like for everybody to see these type of festivals, how everybody mixed together. You wouldn't believe it, you really wouldn't.**"** NEW YORK, SEPTEMBER 1969

"Because a lot of kids from the ghetto or whatever you want to call it, you know, don't have enough money to travel across country to see these different festivals, what they call festivals. I mean seven dollars is a lot of money, you know. So I think more groups, that are supposed to be considered heavy groups, should contribute more to this cause." NEW YORK, SEPTEMBER 1969

"Lots of young people now feel that they're not getting a fair deal. So they revert to something loud and harsh, almost verging on violence. If they didn't go to a concert, they might be going to a riot. Music is such an important thing now. If parents really want to love their kids, they should be aware of their music.

"Well, the idea of non-violence and the idea of when your attendance is over the thing, you should let everybody else in free. Yeah, that idea... yeah. And the idea of people really listening to music over the sky, you know, in such a large body. Everybody thinks that something is gonna go haywire or something, but that's always brought on by the police, always."
NEW YORK, SEPTEMBER 1969

JIMI ONSTAGE AT WINTERLAND, SAN FRANCISCO, OCTOBER 1968

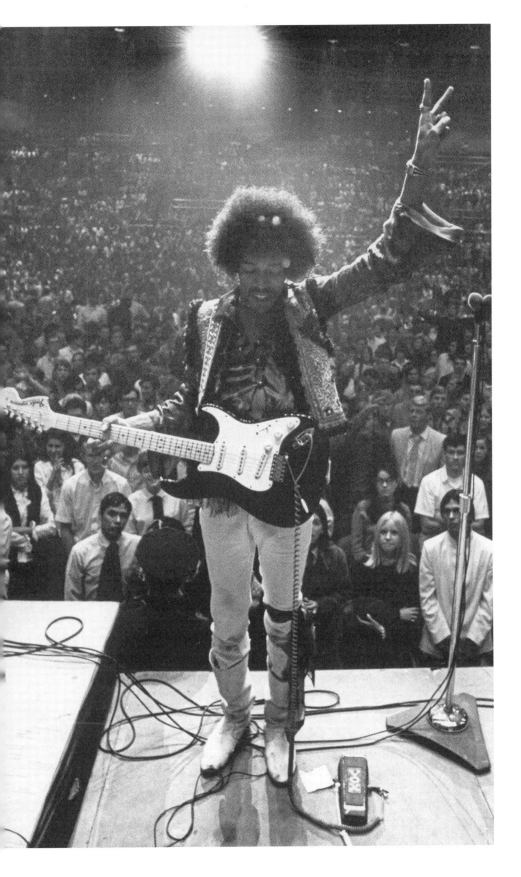

"Woodstock was groovy and all that, but anybody can get a field and put a lot of kids in there and put band after band on. I don't particularly like the idea of group after group. It all starts merging together. They didn't give a damn about the sound equipment. The people way out there that couldn't hear nothing. So when you do festivals you're either going to have to have more days, or offer them more things besides music. You know, you should have little booths where they can buy this and that, where the Indians can come and sell their jewellery. A little circus here and there." **NEW YORK, DECEMBER 1969**

"It's like the money thing of it. Everybody wants to get on the bandwagon. They don't give a damn about those kids out there. If it rains, well it rains. If it does this, well it does this. The way I could see a festival is have a little circus thing over there, have a little tent area, where you have tents you can rent out to folks or whatever. You have music going on at certain times, and then you show films at certain times. You have dances and arts and maybe even a play. Yeah, exhibits and so forth." NEW YORK, DECEMBER 1969

The Star Spangled Banner

"I don't know man, all I did was play it. I'm American so I played it. I used to have to sing it in school, they made me sing it in school, so, it's a flashback." **NEW YORK, SEPTEMBER 1969**

"Oh, because we're all Americans, you know, we're all Americans, aren't we? When it was written then, it was played in a very, very beautiful... what they call beautiful state, you know. Nice and inspiring, you know, your heart throbs and you say 'Great, I'm American!' But nowadays when we play it we don't play it to take away all this greatness that America is supposed to have. But we play it the way the air is in America today. The air is slightly static, isn't it? You know what I mean? So therefore we played it." NEW YORK, SEPTEMBER 1969

"In records, you can do almost anything you want. But then in person, like with the three piece or four piece, you know, with a small group, you're not actually trying to get the same sound, because that's been had on a record. You can leave the concert and go home and play the chord if you want to hear it just like that. We give you another side of it. We play outside, that's another side of it 'cos the air does something to the sounds, and then you can just go on and jam with it. I don't know, it's better playing in person for, I guess, anybody. 'Cos you can just raise hell if you want to."

Jamming

"It's fun to play at little funky clubs, because that's like a work house. It's nice to sweat. I remember we used to play sometimes, even the amplifiers and guitars actually were sweating, everything is sweating. It seemed like the more it got sweaty, the funkier it got and the groovier. Everybody melted together, I guess! And the sound was kicking 'em all in the chest. I dig that! Water and electricity!" **NEW YORK, DECEMBER 1969**

"Far as I like, I like after hour jams, like in a small place, like at a club or something. Then you get another feeling and you get off in another way, you know, with all those people there, you know? You get another feeling and then you mix it in with something else that you get. I don't know. I get more of a dreamier thing

LIFE ON THE ROAD

JIMI HENDRIX *Talking*

from the audience, you know, it's more of a thing that you go off into. You know, you get into such a pitch sometimes that you go off into another thing and, you don't forget about the audience, but you forget about all the paranoia that, you know, you said, 'Oh gosh, I'm on stage, what are we gonna do now?' Then you go off into this other thing. Then it turns out to be like, almost like a play, only in certain ways though, you know, you have to look at it in different ways for instance. **"**

" That's what being a musician's about, it's just playing. Playing anywhere. That's why we can play Madison Square Garden and come down and play at the Experience, then go back over and play the Whiskey and then play Hollywood Bowl. See, once they get all those ideas about what building is which, they're saying, 'Oh, they'll play down there, it might not be very good because they're not known to play there!' That's silly. It's fun anyway to me. It's groovy that we get paid. All the kids have to remember is regardless of where you're going, just check it out. You've gone there to hear the music. It's terrible to have to rely on the Madison Square Garden all the time, 'cos those places are not for real good rock music. Then you have to go to the small clubs and get your ears blasted away. I think that they should make special buildings, like they make special buildings for restaurants and hotels. They should make special buildings for loud, or whatever you want to call it, electronic rock music. **"** NEW YORK, DECEMBER 1969

The Isle Of Wight Pop Festival

" The people were really groovy. The people are very groovy, but I really hate to play at night, you know what I mean? 'Cos you can't see 'em, especially outside. Not too good, I couldn't see everybody and that's what I play off of, first of all the musicians and then second of all the audience. **"** STOCKHOLM, AUGUST 1970

"Well it was so mixed up there and at the time it was so confused that like, I didn't get a chance to really base any... my future of that one gig, you know, except when I played 'God Bless The Queen', [sings] If you know what I mean. And like... I don't know, I couldn't base my whole thing on what I'm gonna do after that, you know, by just that one job there. I was probably happy just to play there, you know. And I was wondering if they was gonna dig us, then quite naturally I'd go on and try to get it together."

LONDON, SEPTEMBER 1970

Concert Admission Prices

"As long as they keep it under ten. I think it should... they shouldn't go any higher than ten shillings. 'Cos after all, it is music and they have to pay twice as much or three times as much to buy the LP."

LONDON, SEPTEMBER 1970

LIFE ON THE ROAD

Guitars & Equipment: Their Uses & Misuses

Guitars

"I use a Fender Stratocaster. Everybody's screaming about the seven-year-old Telecaster, and the twelve-year-old Gibson, and the ninety-two-year-old Les Paul. They've gone into an age bag right now, but it's nothing but a fad. The guitars nowadays play just as good. You know, the salesman is always telling you that Chuck Berry took this one to the bathroom with him and he didn't have no toilet paper, so watch out for the pick guard. The Stratocaster is the best all around guitar for the stuff we're doing. You can get the very bright trebles and the deep bass sound. I tried Telecaster and it only has two sounds, good and bad, and a very weak tone variation. The Guild guitar is very delicate but it has one of the best sounds. I tried one of the new Gibsons, but I literally couldn't play it at all, so I'll stick with Fender." **HOLLYWOOD, AUGUST 1967**

Effects

"Like when we were at the Saville, you know, we used... I had this gadget on the guitar that every time I hit a certain note, the lights would go up, you know." **STOCKHOLM, MAY 1967**

JIMI HENDRIX *Talking*

Amps

❝I really like my old Marshall tube amps... because when it's working properly there's nothing can beat it, nothing in the whole world. It looks like two refrigerators hooked together.❞

HOLLYWOOD, AUGUST 1967

❝I'm getting upset every fucking night because of these damn amplifiers. We're carrying our own, and like, you know, I can't fix an amp, I'm not an amp-repair-man who can get out there. But I know when they're wrong and when they're not. It makes me twice as mad when a road manager tries to tell me... just because they're fogged up, that they're over-working too much.❞

MINNEAPOLIS, NOVEMBER 1968

Jimi On His Own Sound

❝You know, I just turn the amp up very loud and it's mostly feedback and the way you control the knobs and the back, 'cos I play a Fender Stratocaster guitar, you know, and you can take the back off a little small plate and you can tap the springs. There's little springs back there and it makes these weird little sounds sometimes.❞ STOCKHOLM, MAY 1967

❝We just like to play and the sounds that come about, happens most of the time accidental, you know. Like as you grow older, you change slightly without knowing sometimes. And that's what happens to our music sometimes, you know, and I just don't like one style really, I like to play maybe country or blues.❞

STOCKHOLM, MAY 1967

The Sex Angle

❝No, not really. I guess there is some sex, but I don't plan anything. I just do what I feel at the time. Gimmicks? Sure, but we don't work things out, we just let them happen.❞

"Oh, it's good to see people enjoy themselves, regardless of what it is. But what I believe it might be, is like... well, just like you said, it might have something to do with sex, you know, just the idea of somebody being on stage and maybe playing an instrument or singing and you know, showing themselves and... you know, when we're like bowing down and all this and the idea of the people sitting down, knowing that they can't really touch them then, but they would like to, you know, that's a frustrated feeling, but it's a good feeling, you know. They probably don't get a chance to scream all year until this one time and then they let everything out then, you know, this is a chance to let it out." FRANKFURT, MAY 1967

Playing With My Teeth

"Well, you know, I do it just when I feel like it, like, you know. I don't consider myself that I have to do it, you know, 'cos sometimes we don't do it at all. It's just when I feel like doing it."

STOCKHOLM, MAY 1967

GUITARS & EQUIPMENT: THEIR USES & MISUSES

❝It's like playing with your hands like this, you know. You have to move this finger in order to make the notes. So I just, instead of picking it with my left hand, I just pick with my teeth, that's all.❞

STOCKHOLM, MAY 1967

❝It's best not to expect anything from us, you know. It's just best just to go on stage, you know, 'cos to expect something then you might not see it, then quite naturally you're going to be disappointed.**❞ STOCKHOLM, MAY 1967**

Playing Behind My Head

❝I've been playing six or seven years, constantly developing a playing style. Most of it started about four years ago. When I first started, some cat tried to get me to play behind my head, because I never would move too much, you know. I said, 'Oh man, who wants to do all that junk,' and then all of a sudden you start getting bored with yourself.**❞ HOLLYWOOD, AUGUST 1967**

Guitar Smashing

❝If I feel like putting a guitar down and stepping on it, you know, I'll do it if I feel like it.**❞ LONDON, FEBRUARY 1967**

❝There's so many different things we do and nothing is never the same each night, even if it's a bad night or a good night, it's... everything's always different 'cos it's more improvised, you know, almost like a free feeling, you know, free feeling, and everything we do, like playing with our teeth or with our elbows and all that. It's just like, 'cos we feel like it at right at that particular moment.❞ LONDON, FEBRUARY 1967

❝Our show is not stolen. It is never the same. Different with every performance. I haven't rehearsed anything. Everything comes out the way I feel it.**❞ MUNICH, MAY 1967**

"Quite naturally, you have to feel it... in or at least, you know, we mostly feel it, you know, 'cos like if you see our show for instance, once every night for about a week, you know, they'll probably be very different, you know, probably, you know, 'cos it's a different mood you might be in, you know, and the way the music might hit you, you know, it's very, very emotional like. FRANKFURT, MAY 1967

"Like one time I said, 'Maybe I should burn a guitar tonight, I really feel well,' you know? Or maybe I should smash a guitar or something like that. And they says, 'Yeah, yeah!' I said, 'You really do think I should?' They said, 'Yeah, that'd be cool!' So, o.k. So like I just work up enough anger as of where I could do it, you know. But like, I didn't, you know, I didn't think too much of the hype scene and all that because, like I dug, you know, wearing all those different things, you know. It was fun. And I still do, but like I won't see very many other people doing it, so like it has... it gives me a dumb, or a stupid tendency to like hold back from, like my own desires and so forth, for some unknown reason, I don't know.**"**

LONDON, SEPTEMBER 1970

"But like, I didn't know it was anger until they told me that it was, you know, like with the destruction and all that. But I believe everybody should have like a room where they can get rid of all their, you know, all their releases, where they can do a releases at. So my room was a stage."**

LONDON, SEPTEMBER 1970

"Oh it's a thing like when you bring your girlfriend there and you watch us play and so forth, you can get it out of your system then, by watching us do it, make it into a theatrics instead of putting it in the streets. So when you get home with, you know, your family or your girlfriend, so you have all this tension out of the way, you know, it's nothing but a release I guess." NEW YORK, JULY 1969

Amp Smashing

"We don't break things up too much any more. That was only during the frustration period that we was going through. We don't do that too much. We're concentrating on mostly music, you know. We used to do that for publicity and just for our own satisfaction, but then people started taking it the wrong way, they started not appreciating things. They used to come just only to see us, and not to hear us, and that was wrong." BERLIN, JANUARY 1969

"The times we did that, we played about, millions and millions of gigs and when I did this destruct thing maybe about three or four times. It's because we felt like it then. It might have been some personal problem that we might've had, you know, and it comes out maybe on stage, you know, it just come out there."

NEW YORK, JANUARY 1968

"It's just a feeling like, you feel very frustrated and it just comes over, you know, you just go over frustrated and music gets louder and louder and all that, and then you just start thinking about different things and all of a sudden crash-bang! Eventually, you know, everything's up in smoke." NEW YORK, JANUARY 1968

"You couldn't get that together. We did it once before and somebody said, 'That's great! Why don't you plan it out baby?' So, plan what out? I don't know. It just happened, that's all."

NEW YORK, JANUARY 1968

GUITARS & **EQUIPMENT: THEIR USES** & **MISUSES**

Songwriting & the Recordings

Hey Joe

"That record isn't us. The next one's gonna be different. We're working on an LP which will be mainly our own stuff."

"Well, when I was running around the Village, you know, there was... I was starving in the Village, I heard this record by Tim Rose at this club. It was very... You know, I liked it, but, you know, it wasn't being played too much, so I really liked it. So when we went to England it was the first thing we recorded, you know. We put our own arrangement or... you know, on, got it our own way and did it." STOCKHOLM, MAY 1967

"What we're trying to do is, we're trying to get our own particular sound, you know, like a freakish blues with, you know, this rave like almost, only with a little more feeling than what's been happening lately." LONDON, FEBRUARY 1967

"Oh there are so many different outlets, you know, we have so many different things like 'Hey Joe' is just one little... about one hundredth, you know, of our feelings, we liked it that's why we recorded it, you know, but we have so many different other songs, you know, that we haven't even... we just barely begun."

JIMI HENDRIX *Talking*

JIMI HENDRIX *Talking*

Purple Haze

❝Well, it's about this guy. This girl turns this cat on, you know, and he doesn't know which way he's going. But he doesn't know what's happening, really. He doesn't know if it's bad or good, that's all, and he doesn't know if it's no tomorrow or just the end of time for instance.❞ **STOCKHOLM, MAY 1967**

❝You know the song we had named 'Purple Haze'? That was about... it had about a thousand thousand words, and it didn't... it... Ooh! Ooh! It gets me so mad 'cos that isn't even 'Purple Haze,' you know! I don't know, man. I'm just a frustrated old hen, that's all. That's what I feel like. You should have heard it man. I had it written out. It's about going through all these... this land, you know. This mythical... 'cos that's what I like to do is write a lot of mythical scenes. You know, like the history of the wars on Neptune, and all this mess, you know. And the reason why the ring, the rings were there, you know, you have all these... See like how they got the Greek Gods and all that mythology. Well, you can have your own mythology scene. Or write, you know, fiction. Complete fiction though, you know. I mean anybody can say, 'Well I was walking down the street, and I see an elephant floating through the sky.' Well, it has no meaning at all, you know. There's nothing imagining except there's this elephant there, you know, and if you don't watch out you might break your neck! When the shit hit you in your eye.❞ LONDON, DECEMBER 1967

❝I don't consider [it] no invention of psychedelia. It's just asking a lot of questions. It says damn wait a minute I feel... you know, 'scuse me while I do this, you know, for a second. Then, you know, you feel yourself like going in different strange areas and all this, like most curious people do, and I just happen to put it on 'Purple Haze', but the way I write things, I just write them with a clash between reality and fantasy mostly. You have to use fantasy in order to show different sides of reality.❞ **LONDON, SEPTEMBER 1970**

The Wind Cries Mary

❝On 'The Wind Cries Mary', the words came first, you know, the words came first and then the music was so easy to put there. The whole thing just fell in... it just melted together.❞

NEW YORK, JANUARY 1968

❝Well like, the traffic lights turn to blue tomorrow, that means like tomorrow, everything's going to be, you know, blue; blue means feeling bad, you know. In other words, like for instance if you do your every day things, like go across the street or something like that, instead of traffic lights being red and green, well they're just blue, 'cos, you know, in your mind you just... It's just nothing but a story about a break up, you know, just a girl and boy breaking up, that's all. And you know, you just say one thing and you say something like that but, you know, just mean something else.❞ STOCKHOLM, MAY 1967

JIMI RELAXING AT HOME WITH LENNY AND BOB,
MONTAGU SQUARE, LONDON

SONGWRITING & THE RECORDINGS

Are You Experienced LP

❝It has about three or four different moods. It has a little, you know, rock and roll. It has about two rock and roll songs which you can call rock and roll, you know. And then it has maybe... you know, has a blues. Then it has a few freak out tunes, you know. There's the one named 'Are You Experienced' is one. But, you know, that's the name of the... there's the last track on the LP. It's like, you know, imaginary free form, so on, where you just use your mind, where you just imagine with your mind, you know. And this other song named 'Third Stone From The Sun', it's completely imaginable, you know. It's just about these cats coming down and taking over Earth. But then they find out they really don't see anything here that's worth taking, you know, except for chickens, you know. 'Third Stone From The Sun...' It lasts about seven minutes and it's instrumental and these guys coming from another planet, you know. And third stone from the sun is Earth, you know. That's what it is, you know. They have Mercury, Venus and then Earth, and they observe Earth, you know, for a while and they think the smartest animal on the whole Earth is chickens, you know, hens, and so they just... you know, there's nothing else here to offer, they don't like the people so much so they just blow it up at the end, you know. So you have all these different sounds, but all were made from just nothing but a guitar, you know, bass and drums, and then our slowed down voices.❞

STOCKHOLM, MAY 1967

"Many say they can understand themselves better when they take LSD. Rubbish! They're idiots who talk like that."

"I'm already married to my music! You'd have to work a whole lot of voodoo on me to get me married, man!"

"Music is religion for me. There'll be music in the hereafter, too."

"If I feel like putting a guitar down and stepping on it, you know, I'll do it if I feel like it." 🙶

I Don't Live Today

❝On the first LP 'Are You Experienced' you know, well on this track 'I Don't Live Today', there's a guitar taking a solo and it's wah-wah like. But see we're doing it by, with hand then, you know. So then Vox and this other company in the States in California, they made this succeed. The first record I heard with the wah-wah was like, what was that? 'Tales Of Brave Ulysses' by the Cream, which is one of my favourite records. But beforehand, you know, like we used to use a hand wah-wah then, you know, which sounds very good, I think we'll use it some more on records, you know, it's a very groovy sound, it's different than this same ole, you know... We're mostly working with high octaves scene though, it boosts the guitar. Octavia.❞ **LONDON, OCTOBER 1967**

❝**On 'I Don't Live Today' on our LP, 'I Don't Live Today', you know, it's a real, real strong sound, you know. Well, I don't know; the beginning came to me, you know, (sings intro:) dou-dou-dou-dou-dou-dou, you know, and then the music just made me feel like these words. The words and music they go like that.❞**

NEW YORK, JANUARY 1968

If Six Was Nine

❝How could 'If Six Was Nine' be anger? I don't say nothing bad about nobody. It just says, man, let them go on and screw up theirs, just as long as they don't mess with me. Quite naturally, you try to help people out here and there if they can appreciate it.❞

NEW YORK, DECEMBER 1969

Castles Made Of Sand

❝I like to write songs like 'Castles Made Of Sand', personally. When it comes to the ballads, the ballads I really like to get together. That's what I dig.❞ **NEW YORK, DECEMBER 1969**

SONGWRITING & **THE RECORDINGS**

The Burning Of The Midnight Lamp

❝I wrote part of the song on a plane between LA and New York and finished it in the studios in America. There are some very personal things in there, but I think everyone can understand the feeling when you're travelling that no matter what your address, there is no place you can call home.❞

❝It just came to me, you know, that's all. You know, just... like when we was recording our last album LP, you know, and messing around. I can't play no piano, you know, or harpsichord. But anyway, I just picked up these different little notes, you know, and just started from there. But every time we had an intermission, you know, a rest or something like that, then I'd play this little tune on the harpsichord. So we decided to record it after about six months of messing around with it. It's just very personal, you know. You don't mean for the lyrics to be personal all the time, but it is though.❞ STOCKHOLM, SEPTEMBER 1967

❝I really don't care what our records does as far as chart-wise. We had this one that only made number 11, you know. It's named 'The Burning Of The Midnight Lamp', which everybody around here hated. They said that was the worst record, you know. But to me that was the best one we ever made. Not far as recording, 'cos the recording technique was really bad, you know, you couldn't hear the words so good. Probably that's what it was.❞

LONDON, DECEMBER 1967

Axis: Bold As Love LP

❝Well like the axis of the earth, you know, if it changes, well it changes the whole face of the earth, like every few thousand years, you know, And it's like love in a human being, if he really falls in love, deep enough, it'll change him, you know. It might change his whole life so both of them can really go together.❞

STOCKHOLM, JANUARY 1968

"Well axis, like, you know, that's a change, you know, of that scene, you know, so that new civilisation comes every time it changes, you know. And so axis can change the whole scene for us, just like love can, you know, so blah-blah woof-woof. 'Axis: Bold As Love' and all."

LONDON, DECEMBER 1967

"I like the inside cover the best, really, you know. Like they have an Indian painting about us, you know. Well, it's all right, you know, I can hardly wait until the next comes though. The next one will be better."

STOCKHOLM, JANUARY 1968

"But the secret of my sound is largely the electronic genius of our tame boffin, who is known as Roger The Valve [Roger Mayer]. He has rewired my guitars in a special way to produce an individual sound and he has made me a fantastic fuzz-tone, which you can hear to good effect on our new LP, 'Axis: Bold As Love'. Actually, it's more of a sustain than a fuzz. He got a special sound out of the guitar on 'One Rainy Wish' and 'Little Miss Lover'. It come through a whole octave higher so that when playing the high notes, it sometimes sounds like a whistle or flute."

"You make a record. Now when you put a certain sound on the record, or put a certain little freaky thing here or there or something might sound like raindrops reversed and echoed and phased and all this. Well then it's because you're trying to emphasise that certain point in that record. All right then the people only got this in their minds, so when they go see you,

SONGWRITING & THE RECORDINGS

you can have your little tape on, you know. But then the main thing is, the words and all this and they can feel these other little things then. They don't have to necessarily hear them then, you know. But quite naturally we like for them to have it completely like the record and all that. But see we improvise so much on stage, that sometimes a two minute song might come out to be about twenty minutes, maybe. **" NEW YORK, JANUARY 1968**

Gimmicks

"The gimmicks that we do, we don't call them gimmicks because it's part of us; we put a certain sound, like the sound of like planes going through it; that's because we want the people to have such... you know, now that their ears are open for that feeling every sound. **" NEW YORK, JANUARY 1968**

"All those things are all in the mind. All those things that are coming out of us, like we do a lot of those things. Like there's a certain thing on the last LP, on the last track, it's called phasing. It makes us sound like planes are going through your membranes and chromosomes and all this. Well like, you know, a cat got that together accidentally and he turned it on to us like, 'cos that's the sound we wanted and, you know, you hear the sound; but you hit a certain note, you say, well can we... well, you know, there's something we want, it goes Ssshhhhwsshh, and we wanna make it sound like that, but we don't want to use tapes of jet airplanes. We want to have the music itself warped." NEW YORK, JANUARY 1968

"Like, sometimes we play through a Leslie speaker like, you know. And then sometimes you can put that on afterwards or put it on as you play it. It all depends. A lot of times we might play it, we might record with us three or might record as one instrument maybe, and then it's building around there, or either, you know, do us three and then just keep it as three and then put the voices on it, or either sing, you know. There's so many different ways. We don't really have no set pattern actually. **" NEW YORK, JANUARY 1968**

Favourite LP Track

66 Well I'm not sure. It's very hard to say since we have Queen Bee featured on some of them, which is Mitch Mitchell, as we all know. Then we have Bob Dylan's grandmother featured on this – Noel Redding. But I like 'Little Wing' and... let's see, what else do we have on there? Oh, I can't remember the name, what is that? 'Little Wing' and 'You Got Me Floating', I like that one. 99 **LONDON, DECEMBER 1967**

Little Wing

66 Well, that was one song on there we did a lot of sound on, you know. We put the guitar through the Leslie speaker of an organ, and it sounds like jelly bread, you know... It's based on a very, very simple American Indian style, you know, very simple. I got the idea like, when we was in Monterey, and I just happened to... just looking at everything around. So I figured that I take everything I see around and put it maybe in the form of a girl maybe, something like that, you know, and call it 'Little Wing', in other words, just fly away.

Everybody really flying and they's really in a nice mood, like the police and everybody was really great out there. So I just took all these things and put them in one very, very small little matchbox, you know, into a girl and then do it. It was very simple, but I like it though, you know. That's one of the very few ones I like. 99

STOCKHOLM, JANUARY 1968

> **" '**Little Wing' is like one of these beautiful girls that come around sometimes. They might be spaced. They might be, you know, kind of strung out on a certain this or that. You know, everybody has a right to their own releases or their own beliefs, if they want to believe that a star is purple or whatever.**"** NEW YORK, DECEMBER 1969

The Dragon From Carlisle

> **"**There was a song I wrote about two years ago; it's called 'The Dragon From Carlisle' and it had Fat Mattress in it.**"**
>
> **BEVERLY HILLS, JUNE 1969**

Elecric Ladyland LP

> **"**Some of the mix came out kind of muddy, not exactly muddy, but kind of bassey. Because we didn't get a chance to do it completely to the end. We mixed it all, you know, and produced it and all this mess, and then when it was time for them to press it, well quite naturally they screwed up, because they didn't know what we wanted.**" MINNEAPOLIS, NOVEMBER 1968**

> **"I** think it's cloudy. The sound of it, the sound is very, you know, dusty, that's, you know... It's just nothing but going through changes, that's what happens. No well, like Eddie Kramer and myself. All I did was just... we was just there and, you know, make sure it was... the right songs were there whatever, and the sound was there. Not there, but, you know, we wanted a particular sound. It got lost in the cutting, because we went on tour, you know, right before we finished, you know, and actually cut it. There's 3-D sound on there that's being used that you can't even appreciate now, because like they didn't want to cut it properly for it. They thought it was out of phase.**"**
>
> MINNEAPOLIS, NOVEMBER 1968

SONGWRITING & **THE RECORDINGS**

❝Except for 'Watchtower' and 'Burning Of The Midnight Lamp', it was all recorded at Record Plant Studios in New York.❞ **MINNEAPOLIS, NOVEMBER 1968**

❝**Yeah, well actually, we was working, we was getting our things together, and the other two times, you know, with 'Axis' and with, 'Are You Experienced'. But most of those were like, predominantly handled by Chas [Chandler] and all that. But it's the first time we was... you know, I did it by myself completely. It was about, I guess about, sixty thousand dollars, I guess, you know. But well, yeah, it was really expensive because like, we was really recording and was playing at the same time, which is very, you know... it's a whole lotta strain on you, so therefore we always have to go back in the studio again and re-do what we might have done two nights ago, you know. It was really hard to do because, like I said, because, we was working at the same time, and that's twice as much strain on ya.❞** STOCKHOLM, JANUARY 1969

❝Yeah that whole LP means so much, you know. It wasn't just slopped together. Every little thing that you hear on there means something, you know. It's no game that we're playing trying to blow the public's mind or so forth, it's a thing that we really, really mean, you know, it's part of us, another part of us. So then 'Electric Lady' comes along and we really got about half of what we wanted to say then. Oh man it would have taken about two more LPs, you know, it would have been a four LP thing.❞

LONDON, JANUARY 1969

The Nude Cover

❝Yeah well see, we had nothing to do with that, because we've been working so hard and we've been going through a lot of changes in the last two years. That's why we haven't released anything for a while.❞ **HOLLYWOOD, MARCH 1969**

Bad Production Techniques

"It makes me so-o mad, 'cos see that's part of us. And, like, see, like we recorded and everything, and then all of a sudden something happens and it just comes out all screwed up. You just get so mad, you just don't want to know about it any more. Like, our next LP, it's just... every track's gonna have to be right, or else, I'm just gonna, you know, just gonna forget about it. I mean, well, not forget about it, that's the way I feel. You say that, but you're not... But that's the way I feel. Like, it all depends on what you want really. It all depends on where you go to. It really depends on so many things, the cutting of it. Excuse me, the cutting of it depends on, the whole... that's the whole scene. You can get in there and mix and mix and mix, and get such a beautiful sound, and when it's time to cut it, they can just screw it up so bad 'cos they go by levels and all that. Some people don't have imagination. See, when you cut a record, right before it's being printed, excuse me, you know, when you cut the master that... excuse me, if you want a sound where... can... really deep sound, you know, where you have depth, and all this, you must almost re-mix it again, right there at the cutting place. And, ninety-nine per cent don't even do this. They just go and say, 'Oh, yeah, turn it up there, make sure it doesn't go over there. Make sure it doesn't go under,' you know, and there it is. It's nothing but one dimensional."

LONDON, DECEMBER 1967

Recording Costs

"The money doesn't make any difference to me 'cos that's what I make the money for, is to make better things, you know, happen. That's why, I don't have no value of money at all. That's only... my only fault, 'cos I just get the things that I see and want and try to put it into music. I wanna have stereo where it goes up: the sound goes up, and behind, and underneath, you know. But all you can get now is across and across. I'm willing to spend every single penny on it, if I thought it was good enough. But there you go, you know! I do that and then they leave me out there."

LONDON, DECEMBER 1967

SONGWRITING & **THE RECORDINGS**

Little Miss Strange

❝[Noel] he had a song called 'Little Miss Strange'... this is the... it's the beginning track on the A-side. It's the first side of the LP, and he has the beginning track on the side. But like we have him and Mitch is singing this English rock type thing, it's called 'Little Miss Strange', a good song.❞ **VANCOUVER, SEPTEMBER 1968**

Crosstown Traffic

❝I was playing piano on it. And then we sang the background, you know. We're working on more songs that are very hard, but that are very straight to the point, you know. You can always sing about love and different situations of love, but now we're trying to get solutions to all the protests, and, you know, arguments that they're having about the world today. So we'll try to give our own little opinions about that, in very simple words, you know. Anybody can protest, but not too many people can offer a decent answer. So we're gonna try and do that, like we did on 'Are You Experienced'.❞ **STOCKHOLM, JANUARY 1969**

Voodoo Chile

"Like, what we did, we just opened the studio up and all our friends came down, from like after a jam session and all that. We wanted to jam somewhere, but like the studio… we just went to the studio to jam, the best place to jam. And brought about fifty of our friends along." **MINNEAPOLIS, NOVEMBER 1968**

"For instance in 'Voodoo Child (Slight Return)' we used… I was thinking of playing guitar and Mitch play drums and Noel bass, and then I add on maybe two more things. How many tracks is that? That's about… We put drums on three, and sometimes vocal on two and then just spread it out." MINNEAPOLIS, NOVEMBER 1968

"They wanted to film us in the studio. To make this film, 'Make like you're recording boys' one of these scenes, and then so… 'O.K. Let's play this in E there, one a-two and a-three,' and, you know, then we leapt into 'Voodoo Child'."

"Sometimes we pan the echo, what you call pan the echo, so it's going [scccchsch] and that's when you need a twelve track, because you can put the echo on a complete separate track on its own, you know. And then for little different effects here and there, you know. You don't always use up twelve tracks, which will make it sound bigger if you don't, quite naturally"

All Along The Watchtower

"Yeah, all we used on that, well we just used this solo guitar as about er… different types of sounds, you know. Like we used it as slide and then a wah-wah and then we had it straight." **MINNEAPOLIS, NOVEMBER 1968**

SONGWRITING & THE RECORDINGS

Eyes & Imagination

❝There's one song I wrote named, 'Eyes And Imagination', that's the name of it. And it's about fourteen minutes long, but it's about... it's telling about... every sentence or every two sentences, tell a completely different story. It's nothing but imagination. It starts out with this baby crying, you know, a brand new baby has been born, and then you hear these bullets, you know, in the background. You know, it's nothing but just imagination. And it's... every sentence tells a different story, but it goes in about four major movements, but always goes back to this one little theme. You must have that one little theme through it, you know, in the middle, but only enough. There's so many songs I wrote that we haven't even done yet, that we'll probably never do. It's because of... you know, ooh, there's a lot of things around here. Is a really bad scene. You know, we must be Elvis Presley's and rock'n'rolls and Troggs. We must be that. And there'll be no smoking in the gas chamber.❞ **LONDON, DECEMBER 1967**

West Coast Seattle Boy

❝Yeah there's one thing I must admit like, I wrote a... He gave me really a good idea like. I heard some of his tunes, like for instance Bob Dylan's '113th Dream' and so forth and so on. So it gave me an idea to write a song about a... named 'West Coast Seattle Boy' and it goes in... it's very long, you know, it's something about, I've did this and I've did that, blah blah, but, you know, it's something like, you know, but like one line, yeah 'I get stoned and can't go home and they call long distance on the public saxophone' and all this mess, you know, and it goes on to where, you know it's... it just goes on and on. It's like you said man, time is so important now, you know, so many things I want to do.❞ **LONDON, DECEMBER 1967**

Producing

❝Right now, I'm producing the Eire Apparent, which is a hard
rock Irish group. They do more of a tinge of folk in it, just a tinge
of it, but like Irish folk, but it's like hard rock right now.❞

MINNEAPOLIS, NOVEMBER 1968

❝**I love to produce. Not more than music. I'd like to do it when
I can or when I feel like it, you know, whenever I get a chance.**❞

MINNEAPOLIS, NOVEMBER 1968

First Rays Of The New
Rising Sun

❝I'm gonna settle down and record, you know, some nice things, and
then we're gonna, you know... like a single and a LP, or whichever.
I plan to have like two LPs really quick, together, you know, like
maybe about two months apart. Because the second one of this
group's LPs is gonna be called 'The First Ray Of The New Rising
Sun', which will give a few answers I think. You know, every time
we come into town, everybody always looks towards us for some
kind of answer for what's happening to them, you know, and which
is a good feeling, but it's very hard, so therefore I have to live
the life, you know. I have to witness all these bad scenes, and all
these good scenes, so that I can say, 'Well, what I found out,' you
know, instead of just reading books and all that. So therefore I'm
gonna get all these words together in nice heavy songs, very
straightforward songs, you know, and just sock it to 'em,
properly.❞ **SWEDEN, JANUARY 1969**

Freedom

❝We have to go to New York to record on the 1st and 7th to get
our new LP and single together. Yeah, 'Freedom' and 'Both Ways'.
The LP will probably be called 'Freedom' or either 'Band Of Gypsys'
and the single's 'Freedom'.❞ **HOLLYWOOD, MARCH 1969**

Black Gold

❝Mostly it's cartoon material and making up this one cat, he's funny. He goes through these strange scenes, you know. It's all funny I guess, you know. I can't explain it now. You put it to music I guess, just like how you can put blues into music, you know, or whatever.❞ NEW YORK, FEBRUARY 1970

❝I wanted to get into sorta, what you would probably call, just pieces; yeah, pieces behind each other like movements or whatever you call it. I've been writing some of those. But like I was into like writing cartoons mostly, you know. Cartoons, music cartoons. It's in your head. You listen to it and you get some... such funny flashbacks, you know. The music is going along with the story, you know. It's like 'Foxy Lady'. Music and the words go together.❞ NEW YORK, FEBRUARY 1970

❝Well most of the time I hear... I can't get it on the guitar, you know. It's, most of the time you're just laying around day-dreaming or something, you know, and you're hearing all this music, and you just can't... with the guitar. And as a matter of fact, if you try to pick up your guitar and play it, it just spoils the whole, you know, the whole... I don't know, I just can't play guitar that well, you know, to... as to get all this music together, so I just lay around. I wish I could learn how to write and write different instruments. I'm gonna get into that next, I guess.❞

NEW YORK, FEBRUARY 1970

AT THE PREMIERE OF THE JOHN LENNON FILM *HOW I WON THE WAR*, OCTOBER 1967

"Three or four different worlds went by within the wink of an eye. Things were happening. Here was this cat came around called 'Black Gold'. And there was this other cat came around called 'Captain Coconut'. Other people came around. I was all these people. And finally when I went back home; all of a sudden I found myself being a little 'West Coast Seattle' boy for a second. Then all of a sudden, when you're back on the road again, there he goes, he starts going back. That's my life until something else comes about.**"** NEW YORK, DECEMBER 1969

Drifter's Escape

"Oh yeah I liked that, what's that one? Help me in my, what's that? About a drifter or something like that. I can't remember the name of it. That was groovy. I want to do that one. You know, I have the lyrics with me, they were always disappearing all the time. So I guess that was, you know, meant for when I do my log.**"**

NEW YORK, FEBRUARY 1970

Straight Ahead

"We have this one song called 'Straight Ahead' and it says like, power to the people, freedom of the soul, pass it on to the young and old, and we don't give a damn if your hair is short or long, communication's coming on strong and all this kind of stuff.**"**

LONDON, SEPTEMBER 1970

Between Here & Horizons

"Well, I think we're gonna have this thing called 'Horizon', between here and horizon, or something pertaining to that, you know. And like, that goes into certain things like 'Room Full Of Mirrors', that's more of a mental disarrangement that a person might be thinking. This says something about broken glass used to be all in my brain and so forth." **LONDON, SEPTEMBER 1970**

Astro Man

"And then we had other ones called 'Astro Man', he's saying something about... talking about living in peace of mind, well 'Astro Man' will leave you in pieces, and so forth and so on. And 'Valleys Of Neptune Arising'. But all these are psychedelic? I don't even know what that word means, really." **LONDON, SEPTEMBER 1970**

A Room Full Of Mirrors

"Well is, you know, that's reflections like the mirror, you know. Remember that room full of mirrors? That was a song, no it's a recording of the song; anyway, but I don't think we'll ever finish that. I hope not. It's called 'Room Full Of Mirrors', we've been working on it. You're trying to get out of this... you know, it's all about trying to get out of this room full of mirrors."

NEW YORK, FEBRUARY 1970

Singles

"We might have one from the other thing coming out soon though, right. I have this one from Buddy and them, it's called 'Izabella' and the other side is 'Sky Blues Today' is one. And then, I don't know about the Experience though. It's, you know... All depends, you know, the record companies...

SONGWRITING & THE RECORDINGS

they don't release singles anyway, depends what label, you know, you don't just sit there and say, 'Let's make it a track, or let's make this single or something.' They never... we're never even into that. **"**

NEW YORK, FEBRUARY 1970

"You have the whole planned-out LP, and all of a sudden they'll make 'Crosstown Traffic' for instance, a single, and that's coming out of a whole other set. See that LP was... you know, in certain ways of thinking, those sides were planned in order for a certain reason for instance. But then it's almost like a sin for them to take off something in the middle of all that, you know, one-two-three, take out number three and make that a single, and represent US at that particular time, you know. Because they think they'll get more money. They always took off the wrong ones. " NEW YORK, FEBRUARY 1970

Songwriting

"Yeah, I like to get into really good lyrics, you know, 'cos after recording the 'Watchtower' and so forth and then listening to it, then you hear exactly... you know, only through somebody else's words, what you wanted to say at that particular time. **"**

"We have ideas in our mind like, you know, you're at home writing your little song and you say, 'Oh great, then we could have this in there,' you know. And then, you know, you get it together like that. I'm still trying to get that together, you know. All I'm writing is just what I feel, that's all, and not really using too many good... you know, I don't really round it off too good, you know, just keep it almost naked, almost, you know. And like, probably, you know, the words are so bland, blank and everything, that they probably didn't want to get into that. And like when we go to play, you know, you flip around and flash around and everything, and then they're not gonna see nothing but what their eyes see, you know. Forget about their ears. So like, well I was trying to do too many things at the same time, which is my nature, you know. But I was enjoying it, and I still do enjoy it. If I ever... I mean by just thinking about it. " LONDON, SEPTEMBER 1970

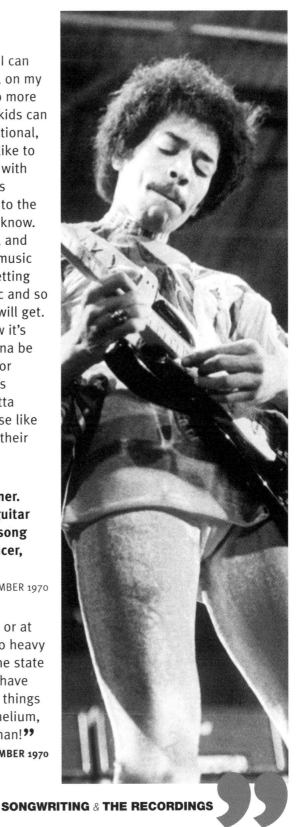

"I'm not no critic, you know, I can just only go by what I want, on my own side. I'd like to get into more symphonic things, so then kids can respect the old music, traditional, you know, like classics. I'd like to mix that in with, you know, with so-called rock today. But it's always changing according to the attitude of the people, you know. When the air is static, loud, and aggressive, that's how the music gets. When the air starts getting peaceful and then harmonic and so forth that's how the music will get. So it's up to the people how it's gonna be. But music is gonna be here, regardless if it's rock or whatever, you know, and it's gonna influence a whole lotta people's minds now, because like I said before, that's part of their church now."

"I just hate to be in one corner. I hate to be put as only a guitar player, or either only as a song writer, or only as a tap dancer, or something like this."

LONDON, SEPTEMBER 1970

"Music is getting, you know, or at least it has been getting too heavy like, you know, almost to the state of unbearable, you know. I have this one little saying; when things get too heavy just call me helium, the lightest known gas to man!"

LONDON, SEPTEMBER 1970

SONGWRITING & THE RECORDINGS

From Religion, Drugs & Girls, to Death & Reincarnation

Religion

❝Music is religion for me. There'll be music in the hereafter, too.❞
BERLIN, JANUARY 1969

❝God? Now let's see, there's several gods I believe in... we have, Noel Bedding, Mitch Mitchell, yes, we have the reincarnation of Thomas Edison.❞ LONDON, DECEMBER 1967

❝Like there's too many people are trying to work with our image instead of listening to the sounds, you know, because we're making Electric... we're in the process of trying to make our music into a religious... well I mean, it's already spiritual anyway and we want it to be respected as such; not to be because of the long hair, because of the red and blue jeans, because of playing between your legs and all that, you know; that nothing but self satisfaction. Our scene is trying to wash people's souls.❞ **HOLLYWOOD, MARCH 1969**

❝All I can just do is what comes natural to me, you know, like, I don't mind... it's a good feeling sometimes when people like... they base a group on maybe your group or something like that.

JIMI HENDRIX *Talking*

But, then quite naturally if they feel, you know, like they want to get their own sound together; well the best thought they have, is to eventually get your own sound together just like what we're doing. We call our music Electric Church music, 'cos it's like a religion to us. Some ladies are like church to us too, which is another scene... oops 'scuse me I'm sorry, watch your old lady. **"**

LONDON, JANUARY 1969

" I don't know, after going to church for a few times and getting thrown out of there because you've got tennis shoes on with a blue and black suit, brown shirt, and then after politics tell you this hog wash about this and that, you know. You decide to say, 'Well let me get my own thing together,' you know; and so music is my scene. My whole life is based around it. So quite naturally it comes to be even more than a religion, and so what I learn, through the experience of it I try to pass on to other people, you know; through our music. So it won't be so hard for them to go around. Like for instance all this violence, people running round through the streets, you know. I can understand their point but like, if they dig the sounds and let the spiritual... It's like church actually, you know. Just like church, how you go to a gospel church; and we're trying to get the same thing through modern day music. **"**

NEW YORK, JULY 1969

" It's just a belief that I have, you know; and it's... We do use electric guitars; everything, you know, is electrified nowadays, you know. So therefore the belief comes into, you know, through electricity to the people, whatever. That's why we play so loud, because it doesn't actually hit through the ear drums, like most groups do nowadays, you know. They say, 'Well we're gonna play loud too, 'cos they're playing loud.' And they got this real shrill sound, you know; that's really hard. We planning for our sound to go inside the soul of the person actually, you know; and see if they can awaken some kind of thing in their minds, you know, 'cos there are so many sleeping people. You can call it that if you want to. **"** NEW YORK, JULY 1969

"A lotta kids, you know, don't find nothing in church. I remember when I got thrown out of church because I had the improper clothes on. I had tennis shoes and a suit and they said, 'Well, that's not proper.' So we don't have no money to get anything else. So I just got thrown out of church anyway, and it's nothing but an institution; so they're not gonna find nothing there. And so then it moves on to trying to find yourself, you know. So therefore you see somebody look  maybe kind of freaky or playing very radical; regardless if it's good or bad, you know, and then quite naturally they take up to this person, or these people... It's up to the people to preach the proper thing to them through the music. You've got to simplify anyway... you know. That's why you have to have some kind of eye dreams on yourself, regardless of what you're like outwards, you know. And then like, once you carry God inside yourself, well then; you're part of Him and he's part of you." **NEW YORK, JULY 1969**

"Everybody should play their own parts. Everybody should be actors in their own sins, as where they write their own scripts. All of the script is coming from God in the first place. It's up to them to play out their parts. There's a physical change coming soon, it's neither bad or good, it's just true. The world's gonna go like topsy-turvy soon. Because humans forgot that they're part of earth-matter, too, and so they have bad vibrations floating around now. So there's gonna be a big physical change."

FROM RELIGION, DRUGS & GIRLS TO DEATH & REINCARNATION

Drugs

❝Many say they can understand themselves better, when they take LSD. Rubbish! They're idiots, who talk like that. If I emphasise... if I were to take LSD, then only for my personal entertainment; for fun or just because it pleases me. But without any psychological reasons.❞

BERLIN, SEPTEMBER 1967

❝Music is a safe type of high. It's more the way it's supposed to be. That's where highness came I guess, from... anyway, it's nothing but rhythm and motion.❞ NEW YORK, DECEMBER 1969

❝Oh, I don't know. Well some people believe that they have to, you know, do this or do that to get into the music. I don't know. I have no opinions at all. Different strokes for different folks! That's all I can say. Sly and the Family Stone I think said that.❞

NEW YORK, SEPTEMBER 1969

❝Well I think probably in the... It was good-time music at first, like I said before, like with Little Richard, Chuck Berry, and Jerry Lee Lewis, and, you know, you can go on down the line; Elvis Presley and so forth. But then like there's a lotta drugs that's dipped into it from the simple fact that a lot of musicians think different than other people; they live different than other people; so therefore they have different releases than other people. It's up to them themselves not to make it into escape. And some of this has seeped in through there. And I think some of the people that were on drugs; some of the regular people, you know... Well like

I say, some of the music seeped in, some of the drug scene seeped in through the music. And, so therefore they felt it was a little better to do these things, you know; like going into LSD or what-have-you."

BEVERLY HILLS, JUNE 1969

Voodoo

"Anyway, there's this girl up there [in Seattle] trying to work roots on me. Work this Voodoo stuff, to keep me there, you know. I had to go to the hospital and all that stuff, but I couldn't make that scene. She tried working roots, you know, that's a scene like; they might put a, you know... there's different things they can do. They can put something in your food, or either put some hair in your shoe, you know, some of their hair in your shoe. Voodoo stuff, yeah, and all that kind of stuff, yeah. Well, she tried that, and I don't know, she must have tried it half-heartedly, 'cos I was only sick in this hospital for about two or three days."

LONDON, DECEMBER 1969

"Like, around in the Southern United States, you know; they have a lot of scenes like that going on. But if I see it happen or if I feel it happen, then I believe it, you know; then not necessarily if I just hear it being talked about. If a person, you know, a person gives off... they give off certain, you know, electric shocks anyway really; they can actually get those things together really, you know; the vibrations are strong enough to get these charms working, you know, they can actually do it." LONDON, DECEMBER 1969

Girls

"I had one [car] back home, but a girlfriend wrecked it. She ran it straight through a hamburger joint. After that, I started to devote more times to my music than to girls."

"Like, if I'll get up at seven o'clock in the morning, and I'm, you know, really sleepy; well then I see... open the door and see someone that appeals to me, you know. Well like... first of all thinking of all the white fleshed... First of all I say, 'What in the world is she doing here,' you know, or, 'What does she, you know, want,' or something like that. As I stand there, she says, 'Oh maybe can I come in.' And I'm standing there and really digging her, you know, she's really nice looking. But to tell the honest to God truth, like... she's about nineteen or twenty or, you know, beyond the age of so and so. And so I say... Well I'll probably stand there, and then; there I go, I'll probably invite 'em in to a nap with me maybe or something, you know. Tell the honest to God truth, that's the way I am, 'cos, I can't... [laugh] When it comes to that." WORCESTER, MASSACHUSETTS, MARCH 1968

"Yeah, she seems like a nice girl; and I'd like to take her home and, you know, scrub her up a little bit, and then, you know, come on to a scene, and then, get the clothes measured up maybe. Oh, that's right, yeah she's supposed to come over here for that anyway. You see, I don't go by... go like... some girls, you know, go by appearances, you go by different... There's other things that girls have to offer besides their looks, you know. That makes you make... might want to be with them, you know, for a second or two, you know... I mean, well, there's other things, you know, besides that, I don't just go by, just looks, you know, 'cos, we know the story, you know, some of them... just one... some of the worst people in the world. But, you know, you go by other things, I don't know what it is. You can just feel the little things. You say, 'damn, I might want to be with her;' I don't know; let me check myself there, see what happens. That's great." LONDON, DECEMBER 1967

"If you're not used to it, it will... can kill you really, you know. Really! But it's another way of communication. That's why other people can't understand and say, 'Well, damn, why are you with so many people?' You know, but I say well I don't necessarily be, you know, touching those people all the time, I'll just be talking to them. Some I talk to, and then others, you know... what... you know, are there for; and there after. This is a scene, like it's... if it's part of you, you know. This is nature. I don't know, I just can't help it, that's all. This is a scene like; that's another way of communication though. You have your own ways, you know. Some people just communicate better by, you know, by not even knowing each other's name, by saying, 'Hey, hi, how are you doing there?' Or, 'Would you come for a beer or for a minute?' And then, you know, and then you do that. And you can be the best of friends then. Some even get married after that. I used to be on the block starving, you know. And girls used to help me and all that, you know. Girls are some of my best friends, because they used to help me, you know, and really help me, too. And I really... Ever since then, that's why I say to myself, wow. Any girl I meet now, I want to show her my appreciation for what they did for me before. No serious though, I don't know, it's just nature."

LONDON, DECEMBER 1967

FROM RELIGION, DRUGS & GIRLS TO DEATH & REINCARNATION

Marriage

❝I almost did that. With music there's no room for anything else. I'm already married to my music! You'd have to work a whole lot of voodoo on me to get me married, man!❞

Death & Reincarnation

❝That's why everybody shouldn't get hung up when it's time for you to die, because all you're doing is just getting rid of that old body, you know. The same old body you've been having for about, what is it, about seven years. People really believe that every single person's born here... is completely different, you know, I mean that's true but, through the times, can you imagine all these... but what if we all was supposed to go to heaven and all that. Can you imagine all these people who died beforehand, and all of us, all up in heaven? All living on top of each other, 'Hey, man, move over man, I don't have no room up here! 'Cos oh hell, you had no business dying did you?' So oh, well, God! So can you imagine that?! Wow!❞ **NEW YORK, SEPTEMBER 1969**

Space Travel

❝Yeah, I never did want to go to the moon too much. I always wanted to go to Saturn or Venus, or something like that; something that could show me some kind of scenery. I believe that maybe in one sense we might be nothing but little ants to them, you know. Quite naturally they might not even want to bother us, you know, they might be on their way to somewhere else. I mean you wouldn't go about two miles out of your way just to step on a ant hill. I don't know what everybody should be scared about though. They should try to get in contact some kind of way. It's very abstract type... but you know, I don't know, I really care not to dream about getting into something and going off, you know, away to somewhere else.❞ **LONDON, DECEMBER 1967**

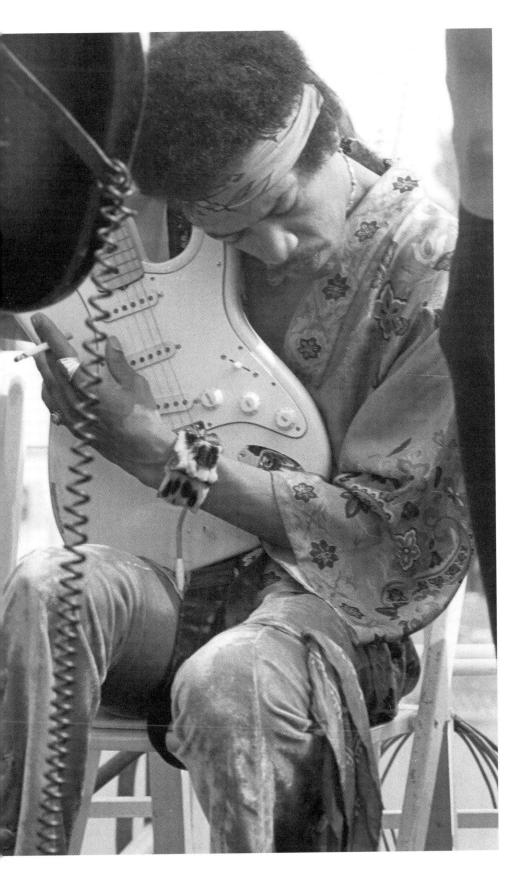

Politics & Style

Personal Philosophy

"Well, let's see, personal philosophy? Well my personal one is that it's part of my life, you know, it's just a part of me; music itself. And the effect I would like to have for it on audiences, maybe in a hypnotic state, if not an awakening state, you know. So therefore, that's why we don't preach necessarily violence, unless it's a certain incidence in a song. It should have some kind of solution, you know, at the end of a song; every song that we give out to the people, you know, 'cos it's all... it's almost all philosophy, our music is... most of it is in a very hazy form, because it's still, it's still progressing, you know. It's just like a little baby, and it hasn't even reached the stage that I call; for it to walk by itself, you know." **BEVERLY HILLS, JUNE 1969**

Riots

"Well, sometimes when there's a lotta riots and so forth; that's still gonna happen in the States, you know, and anywhere else for that matter. So therefore, in the hottest parts of the country, they should allow these groups to play in an outdoor way, you know. I know that sounds suicidal, but it's not at all; matter of fact it's the best way to do anything. Is to bring only special groups though, certain groups; because there's a lot of groups that's trying to... like I said before, keep harmony amongst people. So, they either

JIMI HENDRIX *Talking*

give them good-time music or loud music, so they can release their frustrations and so forth. Standing right next... You know, like black and white standing next to each other with hammers, getting ready to hit each other, and this music has a way... it's a universal language anyway, and if it was respected properly it would have a way to reach these people at the same time. And like, it's a thing like... I think it should be brought outside, almost like the Evangelists, you know, a gathering like that. The other music should stay in clubs and, you know... All the pretentious people in the music, well they should just stay in their pretentious bag, like for instance in clubs and cabarets and all that. But see, there's a lot of elderly people wanna know about what's happening in the new music today too. They wanna know why people play so loud, you know, and they wanna know this and they wanna know that. Well it's the best thing for them to do, is come and hear certain groups. There's only certain groups that are trying to get across a harmony message anyway. And we're one of 'em. **"**

Racism

"The race problem is something crazy. The black riots in American cities, that you can read so much about in the papers currently, are just as crazy. What they are doing is irresponsible. I think that we can also live quietly, side by side. With violence; a problem like that has never been solved. The race problem exists in Europe too. But they don't talk so much about it. **"** **BERLIN, SEPTEMBER 1967**

"I wish they'd had electric guitars in cotton fields back in the good old days. A whole lot of things would have been straightened out. Not just only for the black and white, but I mean for the cause! "

"Well, it's so funny, because even some coloured people look at my music and say, 'Is that white or black?' I say what do you want it... you know, what are you trying to dissect that for? Try to go by the feeling of it. Just because it's loud. **"**

"All those are things that we have to wipe away from the face of the earth, before it can live in harmony."

"Everybody isn't a hang up though, 'cos, that's the human beings, just a bit dumb-sighted anyway, you know. That's naturally... just like how we're gotta fight, you know; like being honest and all that. That's human beings deep down inside, and then nobody can go around and see to all these little boys, you know, like America's little boys, and, you know, all these... the countries to me are like little kids playing with different toys. All of a sudden one little kid runs over to the other, you know, or a little bigger... But see all these countries are still growing up, and pretty soon, you know... and their children come around and do the same, you know. So it's no big thing, you know, really, it's no big problem, because that's human beings anyway, to fight and to compete against each other." NEW YORK, JANUARY 1968

JIMI POSES NEAR THE FIRST LONDON FLAT
HE SHARED WITH MANAGER CHAS CHANDLER

POLITICS & **STYLE**

Militant Groups

"No man, listen. Everybody has wars within themselves, so you form all like... you know, you form different things and it comes out to be war against other people and so forth and so on. But that's what that boils down to. I don't care if you go black or white militant, or Spanish for that matter. Let me say this is or say that."

NEW YORK, FEBRUARY 1970

"Yeah, I naturally feel a part of what they're doing, in certain respects, you know. But everybody has their own ways of saying things. They get justified as they justify others, you know; in their attempts to get personal freedom. That's all it is. Yeah, I'm still free, but not to no, you know, aggression or violence or whatever you want to call it. I'm not for guerrilla warfare."

NEW YORK, FEBRUARY 1970

Politics

"All I know is what I read in the papers. I don't care, so long as they don't drop the bomb before I get a chance to make money."

"It just seems to me that music has a lot of influence on a lot of young people today, you know. Politics are getting... well, I don't know, you know, how they're getting, you know. A cat was talking on TV and a cat in Mississippi, a farmer in Mississippi, can't barely understand him, except when he says 'America,' you know. So then he's gonna vote for him. But it's through music, it's all true, either true or false, you know. And like such a large gathering of people with music, it shows that music must mean something. And then it breaks down to the arts of Earth, you know, the Earth arts." NEW YORK, SEPTEMBER 1969

"Oh, well, I don't know, I might be living in the wrong time, but I don't go by comparisons. I just go by the truthness or the falseness of the whole thing. The intentions of whatever it might be. Forget about comparing, that's where we make our biggest mistakes."

"All it did was bring changes from marked... Even before the times of King, Dr. Luther King, you know. They bring a whole lot of changes. But some people, after this, after the excitement, or the back wash, or the change slows down they say, 'Yeah, well that was groovy. Let's see, what else can we feast upon now?' You know. One of them things. There's a whole lot of changes happening, but now it's time for all these changes to connect."

NEW YORK, SEPTEMBER 1969

"We don't preach violence or aggression. This is a very good thing to have around; it's better than politics, you know. They look up to us sometimes quicker than they'll look up to what the President says, you know. And, you know, well like clothes and so forth, some people just wanna wear these clothes, but that's not harmful at all. That's just a person, you know, he's... him doing his own thing with his clothes and so forth. There's so many things, that people just get misunderstood."

"[Music] It's getting to be more spiritual so than anything now. Pretty soon I believe that they're going to have to rely on music to like get some kind of peace of mind or satisfaction; direction actually. More so than politics, because like politics is really on a evil scene, you know. That's the way I look at it anyway. It's on a big fat evil scene, for instance. It's the art of words, which means nothing, you know. So therefore you have to rely on a more of a earthier substance. Like music or the arts, theatre, you know, acting, painting, whatever." NEW YORK, JULY 1969

POLITICS & STYLE

Vietnam

"Did you send the Americans away, when they landed in Normandy? That was also purely interference. No, but that then was concerning your own skin. The Americans are fighting in Vietnam for the complete free world. As soon as they move out, they'll be at the mercy of the communists. For that matter, the yellow danger (China) should not be under estimated. Of course, war is horrible, but at present, it's still the only guarantee to maintain peace."

LONDON, FEBRUARY 1967

Long Hair

"I feel almost completely lost now sometimes, you know, from almost anything; 'cos, like, when I was staying in Harlem, you know, like I used to go to the clubs and then my hair was very... was really long then, you know, and I had it... like sometimes I might tie it up, or I might do something with it, you know, Cass say 'Oh look at that, Black Jesus' or something, 'Hey whoa, what's this supposed to be,' you know, so oh man, God even in your own section, you know. Like I have friends with me in Harlem, 125th Street, you know; we'd be walking down the street and all of a sudden the cats, girls, old ladies, you know, anybody, they'd just pick me out and say, 'Look at that, whoa what is this a circus or something.'"

LONDON, DECEMBER 1967

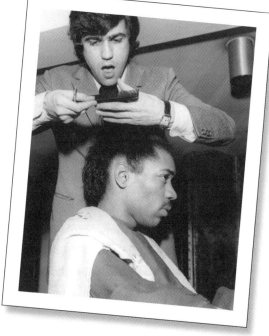

"Well, you know, I don't consider it actually necessary, you know, 'cos there's a lot of groups around like... for instance... well, you know, there's a lot of pop stars around like Engelbert Humperdinck, you know, and Cat Stevens and all the beautiful people, you know; they don't necessarily have to have long hair. It's just... you know, me myself personally, and I believe this goes for the others cats too; is, you know, I dig it, you know, I think it's very nice, you know, especially in your own style and, you know, far as the clothes goes, well, anything I see that I like, regardless of what it looks like, or regardless, you know, how much it costs; if it cost only two shillings, you know, I'll get it if I like it, you know, or if it, you know, if it would suit me or something." FRANKFURT, MAY 1967

"I don't like to be misunderstood by anything or anybody. So if I want to wear a red bandana and turquoise slacks and if I want my hair down to my ankles, well, that's me. They don't know what's running through my blood. Shit, I'm representing everything as far as I'm concerned." **NEW YORK, DECEMBER 1969**

Dislikes

"You know, I do have some, but they'd have to happen before I could really recognise them. They don't bug me unless they really happen." **LONDON, DECEMBER 1967**

Motown

"Well to me, you know, this might bring you down or something like that, but; anyway to me it's like; it's artificial in a very, very commercial and very, very, electronic made, very... you know, what is it, synthetic soul sound. It isn't a real sound of any... you know, like negro artists singing, you know; it's so commercial, and it's so put together, you know, so beautifully that you don't, I don't feel anything from it, except maybe The Isley Brothers who are the only

ones that... and maybe The Four Tops, but far as the rest, this is my own opinion, you know, and all they do is they put a very, very hard beat to it, you know, a very good beat; they put about a thousand people on tambourines and these bells, you know, and they gotta thousand horns, a thousand violins and then a singer, he overdubs his voice millions of times, or he'll sing in an echo chamber full of this and that, and it comes out... you know, to me it comes out so artificial that... you know... but as far as, you know, it has a very good beat and it sounds very good, you know, it's very commercial for the younger people. **" FRANKFURT, MAY 1967**

"It's very primitive thought, you know, it's more like a real foundations thing, it's more like what you can imagine or it's more of a free form type of thing, not exactly necessarily what we're doing, you know, not trying to build up our own type of music, but saying that, you know, that's what I wish we... I hope that work up towards this point 'cos, more of a free style, as it were a person, yeah, quite naturally it has to have a nice beat, but as it were a person can like feel almost into music, you know, how can you feel into music when you hear every single song come out with the same beat and it's so synthetic, you know, synthetic soul's what I call Motown. " FRANKFURT, MAY 1967

Critics

" They are the same people who first laughed. They sat behind their typewriters rubbing their bellies. Now they have turned 'understanding'. I don't think they understand my songs. They live in a different world. My world – that's hunger, it's the slums, raging 'race-hatred', and it is happiness of the kind that you can hold in a hand, nothing more! Maybe the critics suspect a new sound. Still they don't understand my songs. **" MUNICH, MAY 1967**

"I don't care man, I don't care any more what they say any more, it's up to them. If they want to mess up the evening by looking at one thing, you know... because all that is included man, because when I feel like playing with my teeth, I do it because I feel like

JIMI HENDRIX *Talking*

it, you know; all that is complete... when I'm on stage, I'm complete natural, more so than talking to a group of people or something.'"
LONDON, JANUARY 1969

"Oh, I don't know, well I was just playing loud, that's the only difference. No, I don't even let that bother me 'cos they say a lot of things about people that, if they let it bother them, they wouldn't even be around today." **LONDON, SEPTEMBER 1970**

Friends

"Well I don't really know if I have friends or not. I mean the cats in the group and all this, and Chas Chandler my manager and Jerry the road manager. Granny Goose, that's his nickname. Jerry Stickells, Granny Goose. Lot of people I talk to and all that... My eyes are very bad and sometimes you might go into a club and you might not see somebody and they might get all funny, 'Oh you're big time now, you won't want to talk to me.' I said, 'Hello, I was thinking about something. I'm sorry.' Because you day-dream a lot." **LONDON, DECEMBER 1967**

Compliments

"Compliments are not absolutely necessary for me, because mostly they are dishonest. I know myself what's good and what's bad. So I know what to make of compliments." **BERLIN, SEPTEMBER 1967**

"Sometime I have that feeling, like sometimes I might be playing bad and the audience comes up, you know, later on after the gig and pats you on the back and says, 'Man that was great, that was fantastic,' and all this other stuff, you know; well, you know, it makes me feel even worse than it did when I was on stage, because I know exactly where I am as far as playing. That's just the way I think, that just my attitude towards music, it shouldn't be like that all the time, 'cos I could say, 'Well as long as they enjoyed it,' well, you know... but I don't think like that. Quite naturally I care if somebody, you know, knows what we're trying to do, 'cos I don't know yet and I like to talk to that person there, let's see... But like, you know, it's great when people show some kind of enthusiasm, you know, they really get into what we're trying to do sometimes, you know, 'cos we just can't get up there and try to analyse what we play, like say, 'Well we're gonna play this,' and, you know, blah blah, it's gonna be this type of music, you know, we just... sometimes we might play for ourselves and you know, that's on one of the bad nights sometimes, you know, it's a good feeling, when people can really dig what you're trying to do. We don't know what we're going to do at the studio half the time, we don't even know what we're gonna do on stage sometimes. It's just contact between the people sometimes."

NEW YORK, APRIL 1968

"I don't really live on compliments. Matter of fact it has a way of distracting me. I know a whole lot of other musicians and artists that are out there today, you know, they hear all these compliments, they say, 'Wow, I must have been really great!' So they get fat and satisfied and they get lost and they forget about their actual talent that they have and they start living into another world." NEW YORK, JULY 1969

"That's why I hate compliments, you know, compliments are so embarrassing sometimes; 'cos, you know really the truth of what's happening, and sometimes people don't really try to understand, you know. It's like a circus that might come in town, so wow, watch that! You know, and then soon as they fade away, well then they go on and feed upon the next thing, you know. But that's all right, it's just part of life. I'm digging it myself."

NEW YORK, SEPTEMBER 1969

POLITICS & **STYLE** "

Practice

❝Yeah, well I like to, like play to myself, unlike a minute ago. In a room or before we go on stage or something like this; or whenever I feel like... or whenever I feel down or depressed or whatever, you know. I just go and play and... I can't practise though. It's just always constantly; what do you call it? Like a jam, you know. It's hard for me to remember any notes 'cos I'm constantly trying to create other things. That's why I make a lot of mistakes.❞
NEW YORK, SEPTEMBER 1969

JIMI WITH *NME* JOURNALIST, KEITH ALTHAM (LEFT)
AND VIC BRIGGS OF ERIC BURDON AND
THE ANIMALS (RIGHT), ZURICH, MAY 1968

Blues Revival

❝There's no such thing as revival, I'm playing all I know, you know, I'm just playing the way I feel and if it sounds like blues well then call it anything you want; but it's no revival kick, because why go back into the past, you know, why go back there and drag out 'Blue Suede Shoes', just because it's supposed to be hip to revive rock, you know; which is a drag in the first place, because those people done their thing and you know, they're not offering you anything that's very instant are they. There's so many musicians right now playing twenty times better than any Chuck Berry or any Fats Domino or any... I'm not putting these people down, I'm just saying that the music is better now and people just don't even know it. It's right in their faces and everybody accepts it because it's, you know, it's so much better, and they have to have gimmicks and imagery to go by. If they don't have these things to go by, they don't know nothing about music, that's the way some people think, which is a big fat drag sometimes. **" VANCOUVER, SEPTEMBER 1968**

Improvising

" We've been together for two solid years and we've been playing 'Purple Haze' and 'Wind Cries Mary', what is it, 'Hey Joe', 'Foxy Lady'. We've been playing all these songs, which I really think are groovy songs, but we've been playing all these songs for two years, so quite naturally we start improvising here and there and there's other things we want to turn onto the people, you know, as long as they're aware that we're trying to be a music group, regardless of what we might look like. **" VANCOUVER, SEPTEMBER 1968**

Record Buying Public

" I was talking to some little kids, you know, the people that they call teenie boppers, you know. I was talking to them and I found out, and, you know, I just said, 'What was your favourite groups, what's some of your favourite groups, do you know anything about music,' you know, they said, 'Yeah we like Cream, we like your group.' I said, 'Oh [cough] 'scuse me, oh yeah, great, thank you very much.' That's when I said, 'Wow,' you know, their minds are different, so they don't want to hear about this manufactured tin foil music, you know. Right now there's nothing else for them to buy and quite naturally, you know, it has more publicity than most of the best records, so they had to buy something so they buy those things, you know. **" LONDON, JANUARY 1969**

POLITICS & **STYLE**

Sunset Strip

"Well I think it stands for like an escape valve or a place to run away. Some people don't like to live up in the hills, you know, that's just like being hermits and that's running away from something. So they still hold a piece of the city and they consider Sunset Strip of the sort, what do you call it, it's a place to let loose or something like that. And the people might as well own up to this, or well, you know, they might as well face up to this. It's not actually a thing against the establishment, it's not that at all, you know, because a lot of those kids down there. I found out, are part of the establishment, you know. It's nothing but... it's, you know... a lot of them are lazy down there. A lot of them are groovy, you know, but the groovy ones don't preach as hard as the lazy ones do. And so therefore it's a big mess. But clean it up! Running kids away from that is not gonna help anything, you know. You might as well just let it stay there and depend on the music to straighten it out, and then give the music some kind of respect, as of where it can do these things, you know, 'cos police... the more you send police anywhere the more trouble you're gonna have, because some people haven't reached the point of thinking as of where retaliation is not the right, you know, move, specially in aggression." **BEVERLY HILLS, JUNE 1969**

Money

❝I'm so bad when it comes to money. I force myself to save it by not knowing it's around and not being able to get it any time I want. Because I store it away a lot of the time. Because I don't have much value for money except for the things I want, quite naturally.❞ LONDON, DECEMBER 1967

❝Yeah, well sometimes it gets to be really easy to sing the blues when you're supposed to be making all this much money, you know 'cos like money is... it's getting to be out of hand now, you know. And like musicians, especially young cats, you know, they get a chance to make all this money and they say, 'Wow, this is fantastic!' and like I said before, they lose themselves and they forget about the music itself, you know, they forget about their talents, they forget about the other half of them. So therefore you can sing a whole lot of blues. The more money you make, the more blues sometimes you can sing. But the idea is like to, you know, use all these hang-ups and all these different things, you know, as steps in life, you know. It's like drinking coffee... you don't drink it every day, or else you go into another scene with it, you know, like escapes and all this.❞ NEW YORK, JULY 1969

❝Like I want to get up in the morning and just roll over in my bed into an indoor swimming pool, and then swim to the breakfast table, you know, come up for air and get maybe a drink of orange juice

JIMI'S BANK STATEMENT IN THE WINTER OF 1968

or something like that. Then just flop over from the chair into the swimming pool, swim into the bathroom and, you know, go on and shave and whatever. Is that luxurious? I was thinking about a tent, maybe, overhanging a mountain stream." **LONDON, SEPTEMBER 1970**

Protest

"Well the thing is nowadays, anybody can protest, you know, and anybody can write beautiful songs and all that, but some times, if you have a talent where people are noticing you enough, then you should really try to do as much as you possibly can with it, you know. Like, what we're gonna do now, is chop down the words now, and try to make it really tight, and what we're saying is not protesting, but giving the answers of some kind of solution, you know, instead of going towards a negative scene. So that's what I wanna do now, you know, I'm working on that scene, so the next two LPs will be like towards that scene, giving some kind of solution for people to grasp." **LONDON, JANUARY 1969**

"It's up to the people who buy it, they can figure it out, that's all I done, that's all they buy records for, so they can hear things, and they can hear the truth or lies on records." LONDON, JANUARY 1969

Bubblegum Music

"Well they're gonna fade away soon, if all the groups, yeah, if all the groups that make it, you know, all the groups that make a few monies, you know, here and there; well if they should get together and get their own thing together, their own label and all that, pretty soon those things will dwindle out, you know, and pretty soon the public will be so smart as it were, they won't buy those things and do nothing but laugh at them, anyway that's where it's all at, it takes time, everything takes time, but if everybody's honest with themselves, well there you go, it all works out in time." **LONDON, JANUARY 1969**

Solutions

❝What we're trying to do, is get solutions for people, regardless of what bag they might be in. You know, come out of it some kind of way, face up to life a little more true, so they may know to go from there. It doesn't consist of violence or pain, it doesn't consist of any of these things at all. In time of crisis, you know, when you're gonna get these things. That's showing the other side isn't wanting to negotiate. Might as well put it in those terms. But on this side here, there's gonna have to be some people to get off their asses and try to get their selfs together. Instead of sitting around smoke dens, talking about: 'Yeah man, this is groovy. Yeah, protest-protest'. And then come up with no kind of solution. Or if they do come up with a solution, they realise there might be a sacrifice they might have to make like, some cat might have to give up his gig, which he calls 'security', which is a slave thing; that's the worst drug in America today. The thinking, the reaching for it; that's the biggest drug, the worst drug that's happening today. Once you can outlaw that feeling 'security' a whole lot of other things will start happening.❞ **BEVERLY HILLS, JUNE 1969**

❝**Things will happen in time, soon as people give us a chance to work out things by ourselves. Soon as they give us respect. We're writing almost every single minute of the day, or experiencing something. That's the way I live now, because I know what I'm here for. And there's a whole lot of people here who need that one little push, to tell them what they're here for. That's what I'm in the world for.**❞ BEVERLY HILLS, JUNE 1969

❝I was schooled by radio and records. My teachers were common sense and imagination.❞ **BERLIN, JANUARY 1969**

Communication

❝I guess it'd be understanding and communication between the different age brackets. Which is no such thing about age brackets anyway, not in my mind, 'cos a person's not actually old in numbers of years, but how many miles he's travelled, you know, how he keeps his mind active and creative. And I guess that'll be one general idea, there's millions of them though, that can go on.❞ BEVERLY HILLS, JUNE 1969

❝We're trying to get across communication with the old and young and I think some of them are finally understanding that part of it. And plus we try to get across laziness on anybody's part, regardless if they're old and young. And that takes a few more... say a few more songs and a few more gigs to get that across really strong enough. Because like, I used to see a lot of people just sit around and get stoned and not really... all they do is protest and not really, really try to do anything about it, you know. I said, well, listen, you could be a dish washer until you finally get yourself together. They say, yeah, but, you know, ughh! And all this. They don't want to know about that, you know. So I know where the trouble is, a lot of it is laziness. So then I work towards... you know, so then I experience different things, I go through that hang-up myself and then what I find out, I write to other people, because that has nothing to do with aggression or nothing like that anyway 'cos that's just nothing but taking two steps back, you know. And the other people have to realise this too or else they're gonna be fighting for the rest of their lives.❞

POLITICS & **STYLE**

❝We try, but sometimes there's so many things you might want to say in so little time; you get almost like frustrated, like an old maid or something like that some time. That's why you go into these different moods and are very temperamental. I can't help it, because there are so many things I want to do. I don't ever think I'll ever get a chance to do all the things I really want to do, as far as music wise.❞ **LONDON, DECEMBER 1967**

Evolution

❝There's other ways you can settle things, there's other ways how you can live. They're SO block-minded; that's all part of the evolution. See, evolution is of the man, is changing the brain, so quite naturally you're gonna have hang-ups here and there, of thought, you know. But still the whole past is going towards a

higher way of thinking, you know, towards a clearer way of thinking. But there are still some hard-heads just like you're talking about, that think this way because they don't give their selfs a chance to develop in the brain or let the souls develop or the emotions, you know? That's what we're trying to stop from other people, regardless of how old you are, regardless of what age thing. You always have to have that release period, that other side of you, the creative side, regardless of what your gig might be. And pretty soon your job's gonna start to be, not play, but it's gonna start to be more enjoyable too. And therefore... and plus, you know, all this over population, well this is a modern age and they do have pills for this and pills for that. But just make sure those pills are proper, because some of those pills make people sick, you know, you get an after or something, after-effect. **"** BEVERLY HILLS, JUNE 1969

Abortion

"They should legalise abortion. Some of these girls get very sick trying to have babies. And, you know, who says that it's written that people are supposed to... you know, that it's a sin to what-they-call 'Kill off a child?' or something like that. A child isn't a child 'til he comes out into the air, I don't think so. The rest of it, you know... they have to have... think in a higher range of thinking. A lot of young people are and they're gonna get it together. Because a lot of these old people, all they're trying to do; they want to make themselves old, so they tie-up their brains like this, you know. And then they... in the process, they try to build their own heavens, they want to be written down in war history, they want to be written down in money history, you know, all these things. And those things are nothing but jokes. In the next few years they're gonna all be jokes, and those people are gonna be jokes. They're the ones, some of them should be put in cages now to be looked at, because they're getting very rare. **"**

BEVERLY HILLS, JUNE 1969

POLITICS & **STYLE**

The Next Generation

"You got kids coming up, and you don't want them to go to school until they're eighteen and mould away, like you did, do you? Every two years, kids should have certain annual tests. They should have twenty-five pieces of paper to fill out in any way they want to. Every two years, from the time the kid is four. By the time the kid is eleven, if he's a genius, he'll have a chance to stretch out. Put him in special schools. Therefore teachers would have better jobs. The same teacher won't stay in the same bag the rest of his life." **BEVERLY HILLS, JUNE 1969**

A Visual Experience

"Yeah, but see, everybody goes through those stages that... at first... like the first time around and you'd wear all these different things, you know. Like I see some other groups, just like Mountain and Cactus and whatever, you know, like they're getting into them things, so you see the song in new pictures now. Now their hair is getting longer and they're wearing more jewellery and strangling themselves with all these, you know, beads and jewellery and stuff. But it's, I don't know, I just did that 'cos, like I felt like I was being too loud or something, 'cos my nature just changes."
LONDON, SEPTEMBER 1970

"Well I don't want it to be a basically... just only hyped up on all the visual thing, you know. I wanted the people to, like, listen too. I don't know if they were or not though. After a while I started getting aware too much of what was going down. It started to bring me down a little bit, so I just started cutting my hair and rings disappearing one by one." LONDON, SEPTEMBER 1970

Changing The World

"Well, I'd like to take part in it, but change and reality probably, not the way I know it necessarily, but the way that it'd get along a little better as of where old and young don't clash so much together." **LONDON, SEPTEMBER 1970**

"Whatever happens, it should have a chance to be, like brought into the open. If it's a new idea, a new invention, or a new gas, or a new whatever, you know, or a new idea of thinking, it should be brought at least into the open, you know, and be respected as being new and probably, you know, a decent change or a help for the, you know, the human race or whatever. Instead of keep carrying the same old burdens around with you. And you have to be a freak in order to be different, you know. And even freaks, they're very prejudiced. You have to have your hair long and talk in a certain way in order to be with them, you know. And in order to be with the others, you have to have your hair short and wear ties. So we're trying to make a third world happen, you know what I mean?"

LONDON, SEPTEMBER 1970

POLITICS & STYLE

Looking Into the Future

"They're all thinking about their career, and thinking about their future so much. I don't really don't give a damn about my future or career. I just want to make sure I can get out what I want, you know. You know, that's why I say we're very lucky. 'Cos we didn't have... you know, always didn't have that, you know. So, wow, you know, it'd be great if we did really make it nice. But I really wouldn't care, just as long as we could be happy with what we're doing, like recording, and stuff like that. Or do what we want to do. We're still... you know, we're not really doing what we want, we're just, you know, there to please." **AMERICA, DECEMBER 1968**

Astral Travel

"Like, one time I see this deer, you know, and I... 'cos I see a lot of deers around where, you know, where I used to be from. And so, I said wait, there's something that went through me for one split, like I'd seen him before, I mean like... I had some real close connections with that deer for one split second, and then it just went away like that, you know. That happens... you know. Like a lot of friends of mine told me about what happened to him, you know. Have you ever laid in bed, and you was in this complete state where you couldn't move? Or couldn't... or nothing like that. But, you know, you're like that. And you get... feel like you're going

JIMI HENDRIX *Talking*

deeper and deeper into something. Not sleep, but it's something else. But every time I go into that, then I say, 'Oh, hell, I'm scared as hell,' you know, you get all scared and stuff, so you try to say, 'Help, *help*,' you can't move, you can't scream, and you say, 'Help, help.' You gotta get out of it, you know, 'cos you just can't move; it's a very funny feeling. But one time I was going to try it. One time I had that feeling was coming through me, you know, I said, 'Oh here we go,' this time I'm gonna see if I can... I'm just gonna let it happen, and see where I go to, and see what happens, you know. So that was really getting, really scarey man, it's going whizzzzz, like that, you know. And I said, 'I'm not even asleep,' you know; so this is really strange, and somebody knocked on the door, you know, I said 'awwwww'. 'Cos I wanted to find out.**"**

Star Wars

"Do you realise they have inventions now that make it so you don't have to think about defence problems now, forever? They have a plan where they have a laser beam and a chain of satellites around the world. And any rocket released, this will automatically blow it up, anywhere in the world, through a certain chart plan. All this is true; there's scientists working on this now. This is so much of a better idea to spend money on... than to spend all that money on the antiballistic scene, you know, that's nothing but a whole lot of hogwash. He just wants his brothers, sisters, fathers and mothers to have a job, that's all. Scientists are being respected only to keep test tubes clean; that's wrong. Anyway, all this shit comes out through music. We're musicians... I don't know about all that stuff.'**"** **BEVERLY HILLS, JUNE 1969**

Video Cassettes

"I'm thinking about days when finally people will be able to... a lot of people are making more money than they ever had nowadays, so when, they get their flat, they always find their selfs one with the extra room. So like

this whole room can be like the total audio-visual environment type of thing. Like you go in there and you just lay back and the whole thing just blossoms out, with this colour and sound type of scene, you know. Well it's like a destruction room, where you go on... or it's just like a tea room where you go in to have tea. You can go in here and do something like jingle out your nerves or something, you know. And like, well that's, that goes with a cassette, yeah, it goes in with the cassette, you know, you put in your favourite star and all of a sudden this music and the audio, I mean the visual scene comes on. **"**

LONDON, SEPTEMBER 1970

"On stage, if we ever did it any more, stage things with this new band. You know, what I mean, with this new thing, it would have to... it would definitely have to be, you know, audio-visual. And then plus it'd probably only be about five thousand people at a performance, because we'd like to get this geodesic dome and like have the whole thing... just lay it out perfect. It'd probably take a week, you know, when you come into town, like on a train or something, it'll be travelled by train and then it'd take about a day or two, or about three days to set the whole thing up. And then you'd get performance in the next three days or something, of just a handfuls of people coming in, you know. And I think that'll be dynamite. Because then you can work, and then everybody'd get more of an effect from it, you know, instead of putting a big block screen behind you. " LONDON, SEPTEMBER 1970

LOOKING INTO THE FUTURE

Musical Heroes

Otis Redding

❝I almost cry sometimes when I hear Otis's stuff. Stuff like that makes you actually laugh – not laugh from, 'Oh, look at that, ha-ha-ha-ha!' But that real good feeling, and then you get lumps in your throat, and shit. Yeah, that's when the stuff is popping. And if they keep on going, I know I be embarrassed 'cos I know I'm going to cry. I say, 'Oh, no, I got to get out of here!' But they be kicking. That's American, that's American, that scene. Once that's respected, that's what's going to pull America out. The music and the arts, blah-blah, woof-woof.❞ **NEW YORK, DECEMBER 1969**

The Impressions

❝I like The Impressions. I like that touch; I like that flavour; that type of music. It's like an enchanted thing if it's done properly. You see, everybody has their own way of saying things, but The Impressions have been on the right track. They did a thing called 'Keep On Pushing'. They did some really old songs back in there. They're some people that need to be really, really respected. See, these are classical composers. I don't care what their music sounds like today, because today, as things are happening at that particular time, the people that's in that particular time don't really know the value of it until it dies off. But now people really have to start learning the value of things as they're living today.❞

NEW YORK, DECEMBER 1969

JIMI AT THE VARIETY CLUB AWARDS,
LONDON, MAY 1967

JIMI HENDRIX *Talking*

Eric Clapton

❝I've played with him and he's good. It's difficult to compare us, because our styles are so different. He plays the B.B. King type of thing. My main thing is the blues; but people like Elmore James and a few others the people here wouldn't know.❞

WITH ERIC CLAPTON AT THE SPEAKEASY CLUB, LONDON 1967

❝Eric Clapton, I heard him really play once, you know. And see, all these things, I don't care what... you know, like I said before, it just all depends on how your ears are together and how your mind is. Where your head's at.❞

❝I like some of the things that Albert King does. And Eric Clapton, he's very good in some of the things, you know. But I don't have no favourites. Some people like any musician because... like it's so hard, 'cos there's so many different categories and so many different styles going around now. It's so bad to put everybody in the same, you know, bag.❞ **NEW YORK, JANUARY 1968**

Roland Kirk

"We like to hear almost anybody. Well I always tend towards the blues as far as guitar players, you know. I like things from Bach to Roland Kirk."

"He hasn't even started yet, Roland Kirk, and we haven't even started yet either, you know. He hasn't really even started yet. That cat really... when you hear it, you can hear so much for the future too. You can hear some of the things he's gonna go into. I mean not necessarily by notes, but you can hear it by feelings." NEW YORK, JANUARY 1968

"Running through a field, an everlasting field of beautiful things man. You just see that and think, 'That's it, great!' But then you see this over here and then they... oh it's just great, you know, so much happening, especially if you have an open mind for music. Because music is an art, as we all know, one of those scenes what can happen." NEW YORK, JANUARY 1968

"Oh yeah, I had a jam with him at Ronnie Scott's in England, in London, and it was, you know, what else can you say, because it's... you know, I really got off. He was great. He was really great. It was... you know, I was so scared! you know. It's really funny. Yeah! I mean, you know, Roland, [laughs] Roland Kirk. I mean the cat he gets all those sounds and so forth. I might just hit one note and it might be interfering and... you know. But like we got along great, I thought. He told me I should have turned it up or something."

"I like to listen to... to tell the truth, you know, I listen to anybody, as long as it doesn't bore me." NEW YORK, JANUARY 1968

Mike Bloomfield Band

"The Bloomfield Band, which is ridiculously outasight; they're going through all these cuts; they won't even feel what they're doing,

MUSICAL HEROES

regardless of what colour the eyes or armpits might be, you know. And I say o.k. Paul Butterfield, o.k. you know. Let's go... we got this white cat down in the Village man, playing harmonica really funky. So o.k. then. We'll ALL go down the Village man, and hear Paul Butterfield, and WOW! Wow, it turned me on so much. I said WOW! FLIP THAT! And he was really deep into it, you know, he really was, nobody could touch him then because he was in his own little scene right then, he was so happy. **99 NEW YORK, JANUARY 1968**

Chuck Berry

66 Like the Chuck Berry scene, I'd feel guilty in that case, like if we did something like that. I mean, like every single song, use the same background, just you only use different words. That shows that you're only going towards the word scene then... you know. But like, we're trying to cover... you know. It's like anybody who's hungry, you know, what I mean by that is young and wants to do this and that, you know, and also get into music itself, anybody like that, they gotta go into so many different bags and they gotta so much be influenced by so many different things, the whole world. **99 NEW YORK, JANUARY 1968**

CHUCK BERRY

Bob Dylan

66 Bob Dylan, you know, he's been in this business actually for ages, and he's really out-of-sight 'cos there's a lot of personal things, you know, you just don't want to put a whole lot of junk on top of it, like violins and stuff for a certain number, unless it calls for it.

I was his manager with the spots on the street, you know. Like, they're some people... like there's some songs that you do, like, if you're going to do somebody else's songs, most people do it and say, 'Well this is popular now. Well guess we'll do this,' but everybody knows that 'Like A Rolling Stone' isn't popular now. It's a certain respect you might have. You know you just don't do everybody's songs and if you're going to do 'em well, like you don't necessarily have to copy it like them. If you really dig the person and really, really dig the song, well then you do it your own way. I like the way we do 'Rolling Stone' myself.**" LONDON, DECEMBER 1967**

Burrito Brothers

"Who's the guitar player with The Burrito Brothers? [Sneaky Pete Kleinow] That cat, that guy is... oh, I dig him. Listen to him in a... down the Village. He's really marvellous with a guitar, that's what makes me listen to that, it's the music thing. Hello Walls. Hear that one? Hello Walls? Hillbilly have your eye out.**" NEW YORK, FEBRUARY 1970**

Chicago Transit Authority

"Chicago Transit Authority is fun. Oh! In person, listen, that's when you have to hear them, that's when you should hear them. That's the only time. They just started recording, you know. But in person you have to catch 'em though, the next second chance I get is... you know check 'em out.**" NEW YORK, FEBRUARY 1970**

The Band

"The Band? It's there, you know, they got their own thing, you know, together. It takes you a certain place. It takes you, you know, where they want to go [laughs], where they want to.**"**

NEW YORK, FEBRUARY 1970

MUSICAL HEROES

Influences

❝I listen to everything that's written. It keeps my interest. From rock to The Beatles to Muddy Waters to Elmore James which is a blues guitar and singer. And I listen to Bob Dylan.❞ **LONDON, DECEMBER 1967**

❝**Elmore James, Muddy Waters, Albert King. You could also say that I'm inspired by Bob Dylan and Brian Jones.**❞

BERLIN, SEPTEMBER 1967

❝There is no best guitarist. There are so many different styles in music. It's a matter of taste. Everybody should have his own example. I like the style of Muddy Waters, because he plays the 'blues'.❞ **MUNICH, MAY 1967**

❝**This is all I can play is what I'm playing. But I'd like to get something together with like a Handel and Bach, Muddy Waters, flamenco type of thing together. If I can get that sound. [laughs] Or If I could get that sound, yeah, I'd be happy.**❞

NEW YORK, FEBRUARY 1970

WITH TOURING MATES CAT STEVENS, GARY LEEDS (OF THE WALKER BROTHERS) AND ENGLEBERT HUMPEDINCK, MARCH 1967